GUY L. DUNSCOMB

Foot tapping on the footboard of a sweat-stained 4-6-2 at the Tracy roundhouse, eager to inspect the shiny new diesels crowding SP 3122 and her sisters in steam off garden tracks everywhere in Northern California, a tow-headed 4-year-old smiles into his father's camera, squinting in the hot sunlight of Labor Day, 1953. Twenty one summers earlier, SP 3107 provided Dad with his first locomotive photograph, sparking a lifelong association with the railroad both avocational and professional. Now, only one 3100 remains on the roster, and it's Dad's turn to pass on a family tradition. Don Dunscomb and father Guy create a timeless tribute to the shared excitement central to the experience of everyone growing up with trains.

ALBERT C. PHELPS

GROWING UP WITH TRAINS II

A Northern California Album

Interurbans Special 88

By Richard Steinheimer and Ted Benson

INTERURBAN PRESS
Glendale, California • 1983

FRONTISPIECE:

If you're a young woman named Ellen Sparks, growing up with trains means having your dad get you down to the station early in the morning to see him bring in the new *City of San Francisco* on its first test run. You are at Auburn, in December 1936, and it is a Western Union messenger boy who takes your picture . . . Albert C. Phelps.

FRONT COVER PHOTO:

Photographer Dick Dorn and his dog, Tarke, wade through the deep snow of Donner Pass to catch Amtrak's *San Francisco Zephyr* dropping down the grade toward Emigrant Gap.
RICHARD STEINHEIMER

BACK COVER PHOTO:

In a classic view of Northern California railroading by Dick Dorn, an SP director's special highballs past Mount Shasta at Andesite in the summer of 1977.
PHOTO BY DICK DORN

GROWING UP WITH TRAINS II

© 1983 by Richard Steinheimer and Ted Benson
All rights reserved. No part of this book may be used or reproduced without written permission from the publisher.

First printing: Fall 1983
ISBN 0-916374-59-9
Printed and bound in the United States of America

Published by INTERURBAN PRESS
P. O. Box 6444
Glendale, California 91205

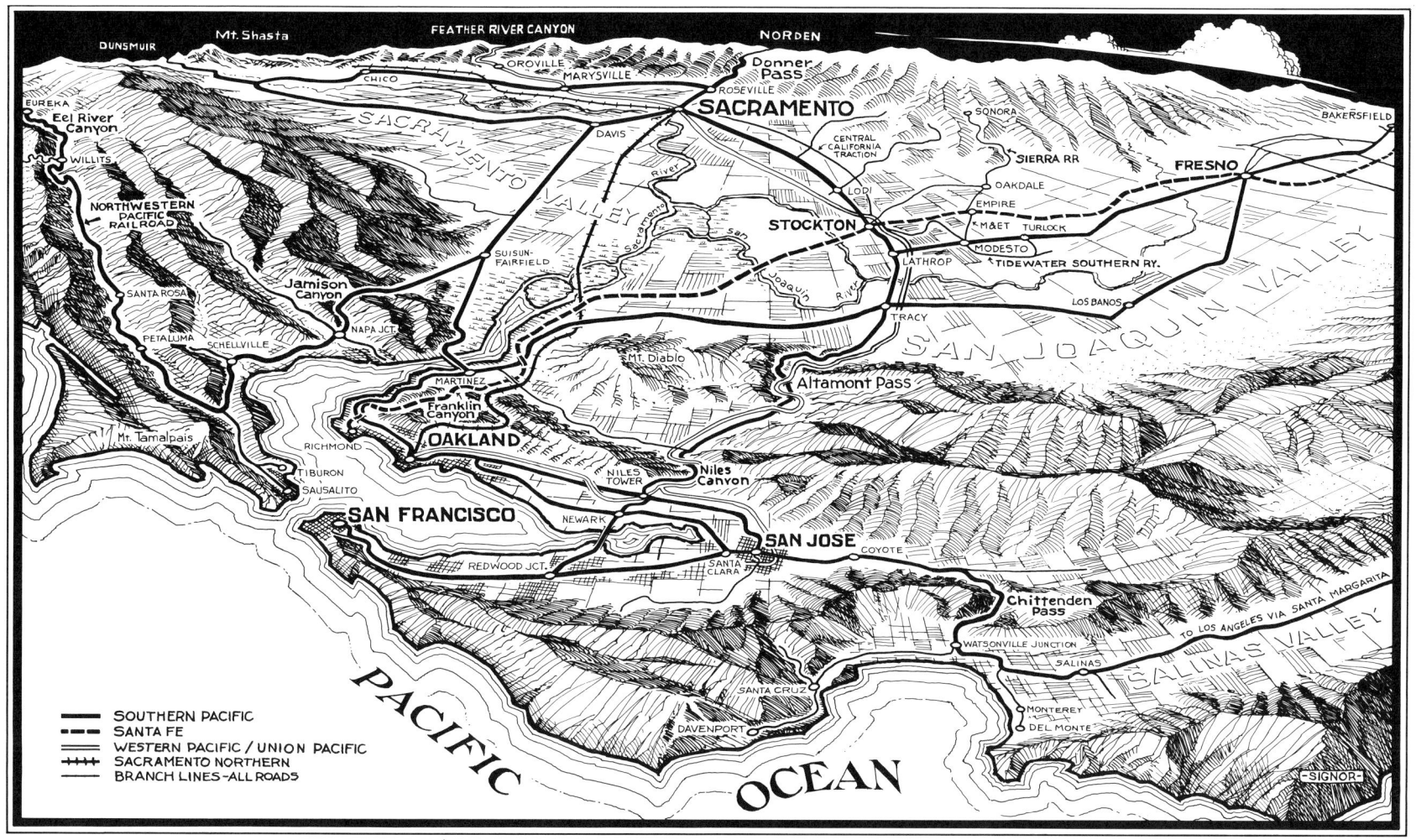

CONTENTS

Introduction 6
Railfan Genesis 10
Golden Gateway 14
Great Valley 46
The Mountains 64
Color Favorites 97

INTRODUCTION

LOOKING BACK, THE SEEDS of *Growing Up With Trains, A Southern California Album*, written with Donald Sims, were planted in my mind outside London in 1980 at Clapham Junction. Glancing out of my coach window at all those youthful "train spotters" at the world's busiest station impressed me with the universality of liking trains.

In this book we'll take you on a spin around Northern California over the last five decades, touching down here and there to see the trains that people loved, and to learn a little about some of the fans who took the pictures.

The 16 pages of color give us the chance to add another dimension to our appreciation of trains, and the chance to try out some personal color layout ideas.

The strength of a picture book resides with its contributors, the people who went out and did the hard part of the job so that we can simply enjoy their images. The credit belongs to them. Additional help for this volume came from Harre Demoro of San Francisco, Dawn Letson of the DeGolyer Library at Southern Methodist University in Dallas, Texas, and John Signor, who used his talents to provide the Northern California map.

I like trains and feel you can "grow up with trains" at any age, anyplace. In fact, I hope fans in other areas will consider producing works along this line. Wouldn't it be fun to see what it means to people to grow up with trains in New England, or the South?
                                    RICHARD STEINHEIMER

"ALL THAT AND trains too!"

Don Sims' introduction to the first volume of this series parallels shared sentiments about railroading in my own back yard. Living two hours away from Sierra peaks and Pacific shores in a community called home by people like Guy Dunscomb and Al Rose was a blessing I didn't fully appreciate until being invited to join in producing this book.

Growing up with trains recalls my father taking me to see steam *Daylights* on Sundays after church, reading TRAINS Magazine by flashlight under bedcovers at night and lying awake until SP's *West Coast* whistled into town. Growing up with trains was chasing the Tidewater Southern on a bicycle, capturing the image on 19¢ film in a plastic camera and turning those raw first impressions into equally raw prints in Tom Taylor's laundry room. Growing up with trains meant taking the girl next door on a first out-of-town date to ride an SN excursion at the Rio Vista Junction trolley museum, falling in love (with the girl, not just the trains) and ultimately knowing the joy of taking our children on trips as they begin growing up with their own new world of trains.

In the ever-changing world of railroading, growth never ends. Yesterday's unthinkable event is often tomorrow's headline news. Capturing the excitement shared by all railfans can be a frustrating effort at best. Still, it's an effort worth making. A blessing's no blessing at all if you don't pass it on.
                                    TED BENSON

THE PHOTOGRAPHERS

Some of our contributors now step from behind their cameras to be recognized, all heroes in the battle to preserve images of our great railroad heritage. The late Art Alter is pictured at Marysville on an excursion in 1940 next to a car from one of his favorite electric railroads. All the other photographers are still active, sharing the same hobby in diverse and individualistic ways.

Ted Benson

Art Alter

Dave Stanley

Wilbur Whittaker

Albert C. Phelps

Don Buchholz

Tom Taylor

Kyle Brehm

Jeff Brouws

Paul Lukens

Tom Savio

RICHARD STEINHEIMER
Alfred Haij

Harre Demoro

RICHARD STEINHEIMER
Guy Dunscomb

CURTIS FUKUDA
Bruce MacGregor and Richard Steinheimer

RAILFAN GENESIS

AS CONTRIBUTIONS FOR *Growing Up With Trains II* gathered in the summer of 1983, Jeff Moreau, Tiburon publisher and life-long railfan, suggested we mention the beginnings of the railfan movement in Northern California, a rich heritage as diverse as the region's railroads.

"You might be surprised to learn that early in this century it was considered almost insane to declare an interest in American trains, or worse yet, streetcars. Anything more than casual curiosity about railroads was something to hide. People were shunned and disinherited for an interest in something so prosaic and so much a necessary evil of that period," Moreau noted.

Indeed, railfan photography in Northern California didn't seem to begin until the 1890s with the photographs of L. S. Slevin of the Monterey area. After the turn of the century he was joined by a Bay Area resident, Robert McFarland. Men like W. J. Bullus, W. E. Gardiner, Stanley W. Keefe and Reubin E. Hill made trolley photos in a seeming void. The only railfan known to actually earn part of his living taking pictures for a railroad was David L. Joslyn of SP's Sacramento General Shops.

Things began to change around 1920. Ralph W. Demoro, a pharmacist at the Ferry Building in San Francisco began shooting, and he was joined by L. I. Bonney, Frank Fennell, Waldemar Sievers and Eddie Young. As rail service began eroding in the 1930s, the early fans discovered they weren't alone.

"I thought I was the only weirdo in the world who took train pictures until I ran into Guy Dunscomb at the West Oakland roundhouse," Jim Boynton recalls. "Guy felt the same way until he met me."

Through the International Engine Picture Club in *Railroad Man's Magazine*, fans began meeting each other. Grahame Hardy's bookstore in Oakland became a gathering place; rail books and railroadiana eventually crowding out more "legitimate" items as fans began to organize into groups like the California-Nevada Railroad Historical Society and the Northern California Railroad Club. At first, C-NRRHS was just a letterhead used by Hardy and WP engineman Bill Pennington to talk obliging railroads out of old photographs and paper goods.

By 1937, when Gilbert Kneiss helped start the Pacific Coast Chapter of the Railway & Locomotive Historical Society, enough interest was detected to warrant the operation of railfan excursion trains. The Nevada County Narrow Gauge and the Sierra Railway trips the two clubs sponsored were the first railroad fan trips in the West.

By the end of WWII, railfan groups were firmly established, running special trains, saving antiquated pieces of rolling stock and recording industrial history with ink and silver halide.

Writing for publication and photography have always been the most visible areas of the railroad hobby. Grahame Hardy, and his partner, Ted Wurm, published three of the early books by Lucius Beebe and Charles

WILBUR C. WHITTAKER

It is all-aboard at Colfax on May 23, 1937, for the first railroad fan trip west of the Mississippi organized personally by Gilbert Kneiss of the R&LHS. Get aboard that train with your box cameras and Graflexes for the 25-mile Nevada County Narrow Gauge Railroad trip to Nevada City . . . the trip that really launches the fan movement in Northern California and the West.

Clegg, opening the eyes of the public to the history and romance of railroading. Beebe, the talented, eccentric newspaperman, with Charles Clegg, created the modern railroad action book, and helped to make the hobby respectable for all fans. Beebe's poetic prose and Clegg's larger-than-life approach to rail photography had profound impact on generations of photographers and writers, including the authors of this book.

In more technical realms, research standards of national historical groups have been greatly advanced by the efforts of Guy Dunscomb, Harre W. Demoro, David Myrick, Fred Stindt and Charles Smallwood. The works of Northern California authors such as Gilbert Kneiss, Robert Hanft, Bruce MacGregor and Ted Wurm blend solid technical information with a broad historical narrative that considers the role of railroading in the society it serves.

With the growing number of photographers and publications, collectors like Randolph Brandt, Roy D. Graves, Warren E. Miller, Bob and Louis Stein and Vernon J. Sappers preserve invaluable contributions to the visual history of Northern California railroading.

Contemporary regional news publications such as *CTC Board*, *Rail Travel News*, and *Pacific News* owe much to the 1930s high school student, Francis A. Guido, who, with partners, started *The Western Railroader*. This original "rough draft of railroad history" is still going strong. Today, one only needs to read the magazine ads for movies, slides, photographs, records, audio and video cassettes to realize that the railfan information explosion is just beginning.

Beyond all this documentation lies the collection of the physical artifacts of Northern California's rail heritage. Rail equipment is preserved *and* operated by groups such as the Bay Area Electric Railroad Association and the Pacific Locomotive Association. The California State Railroad Museum in Old Sacramento, a world class transportation exhibition, is an outstanding tribute to the efforts of Kneiss, Stindt and other tireless R&LHS members who were actively soliciting equipment donations at a time when it was more patriotic to melt down Old Engine Number Nine to shoot back at the Germans and Japanese. Most of our "prosaic" heritage would have been lost without the efforts of preservation groups such as these.

At the front lines of the industry itself we find the true renaissance figures in railfanning, the people sufficiently interested in the profession to seek its employment and put their interests to work for the future of railroading. As the names of Baer, Flynn, Kuhn, Meeker, Schmid and Stanley climb the seniority rosters, supplanting Boynton, Dunscomb, Lloyd, Josserand, Pennington and Phelps before them, the tradition of "living the faith" continues as it has for the last 80 years. Considering the transitional nature of railroading in the 1980s, this kind of devotion is remarkable indeed.

The devoted sharing and caring of the vast majority of the fans from all generations creates the hobby we enjoy today. It is something positive and enduring at a time when such values seem outdated and corny to most people. Ours is a bond shared by all ages, genders, colors and beliefs; people who might have nothing more in common than a love of trains can share in an example of democracy most pure and free as a result of that interest.

In this day and age, such ideas *are* almost insane.

RICHARD STEINHEIMER/DEGOLYER LIBRARY

TED WURM COLLECTION

RICHARD STEINHEIMER PHOTOS

After the first Western fan trip in May 1937, Northern California fans started moving fast. Six unlikely looking characters (above) stand at Placerville on a club trip over the Michigan-California Lumber Company. From left are: Marvin Maynard, Jim Boynton, Ted Wurm, Bob Searle, George Henderson and Doug Richter.

Helping to make the 1950s memorable (opposite) were the McCloud River Railroad trips. The #25 is showing off at the top of the hill above McCloud, only to break down a few moments later and require a diesel "rescue."

The top talent is around (right) in 1983 for San Francisco Trolley Days. From left are Tom Gray, Dale Sanders, Doug Richter, Harry Peat, Al Rose, Wilbur C. Whittaker, Dave Stanley, Guy Dunscomb, Jeff Moreau, Fred Stindt and Chuck Ditlefsen. Some fan trips are behind diesel power, as on this Northwestern Pacific excursion in the 1950s (upper right) with Peter Strittmatter, Bruce and Doug Ketron enjoying the scenery.

GOLDEN GATEWAY

THE FOG-FILTERED LIGHT of late afternoon catches Southern Pacific P-10 2484 treading lightly over the still backwaters of the Pacific-type's namesake ocean at Oakland Pier, the semi-streamlined 4-6-2 heading for the barn at West Oakland after the afternoon sprint from San Jose on train 255, the *Coast Daylight*'s East Bay connection. It is fitting that a railfan's tour of Northern California begin here, for it was into these waters that the first treasure hunters sailed in 1849, dreams focused on a Golden State where precious metals washed over granite streambeds free for the finding. With the first wave of national awareness came the underlying need for a transcontinental transportation system to link the waters of East and West and a half-century of railroad building by companies whose last name always seemed to be "Pacific."

Completion of that First Transcontinental Railroad provided superior travel options for those weary of the months-long voyage around Cape Horn and the perilous land-sea shortcut over the Isthmus of Panama, whose disease-ridden jungles claimed the life of the Chief Engineer of that first transcontinental rail system. Eventually, the rails that led iron horses down to drink by Pacific waters branched out from San Francisco Bay, opening the Golden Empire to immigrants seeking more than fleeting fortune. To the south, the rails tapped rich farmland in the Salinas Valley before scaling the Santa Lucias to reach San Luis Obispo and the 113 miles of shoreline running leading to the City of Angels. To the north, the rails wound reverently through an avenue of giant redwoods to arrive in a land some consider the 51st state in a nation of 50, opening the forest to countless boardfeet of timber production while attracting a stream of summer pilgrims to ponder trees alive and flourishing at the time Christ and His Disciples walked the earth with a message as peaceful and comforting as the tranquility of late afternoon in a quiet sequoia grove.

By the time the Rush of '49 marked its centennial, steam power like SP 2484 faced a sunset no bank of Bay fog could hold at bay. Oakland Pier's ferry connection to the City was equally doomed, the ferryboats' futures and the futures of trains like the little *Oakland Daylight* predetermined by the automobiles whose all-pervasiveness created the need for the steel of the Bay Bridge spanning the horizon. Some 35 years after a young City College of San Francisco photography student made the negative of SP 2484 on an afternoon redolent with creosote and salt breeze, change continues to be a fact of life for Northern California railroads, restructuring to face a future vastly different from their perfumed yesterdays.

RICHARD STEINHEIMER

Mornings in the twilight years on Oakland Pier saw great changes in progress, a colorful time unmatched by any previous era at the "Mole." Skyline casing atop her boiler carrying a building pillar of exhaust over the trainshed and out to sea, Mt-4 4-8-2 4363 takes the Los Angeles-bound *San Joaquin Daylight* down Track 10 beside train 10's dieselized consist, the clean 7:30 AM sun reflecting red and orange in unbroken bands as the company-constructed motive power of 1929 enters the 1950s with a presence belying her years, cannonading into the dawn as if steam would live forever.

Forty-five minutes after 52's departure, it is train time for 10 on 9; a half-hour before departure, the new *Shasta Daylight* loads passengers for Portland on SP's longest daylight (and then some) journey. Past the first stop at Martinez, breakfast patrons in the coffee shop car hardly notice any slackening of the pace of the Alco PA/PB units leading Number 10 up the 0.9% approach to the Carquinez Strait crossing, aromas of diesel smoke and frying bacon mixing with the "eau d' Mococco" emanating from the many trackside oil refineries providing Martinez with a solid industrial base in the blossoming Internal Combustion Age.

ALL PHOTOS: RICHARD STEINHEIMER

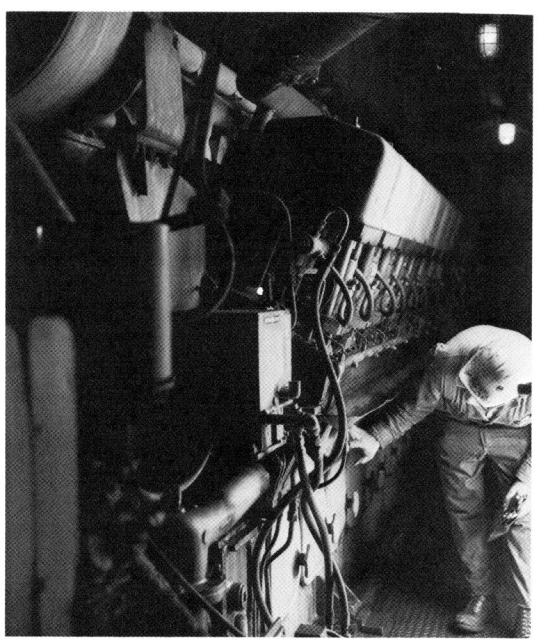

Heralded in their own twilight years as "honorary steam locomotives," the handsome Alco passenger diesels gathered in a tight circle at Oakland like the internal expansion brethren before them, working in dedicated service oblivious to newer generations of motive power. Such dedication meant a madhouse of activity on the West Oakland diesel "launch pad," where incoming Alcos off *City of San Francisco* 101 had but 90 minutes for inspection, refueling and running repairs before the head brakeman was checking the indicators for Number 102 and the blue flags came down for another turn back over the Sierra to Ogden. Departure from Oakland 16th. Street Station with a *City* bolstered by overflow traffic during the airline strike in summer 1966 found five PAs winding up their lagging turbochargers in a display that would have humiliated a good steam fireman. Trackside photographers had a hard time keeping the grins off their faces.

ALL PHOTOS: RICHARD STEINHEIMER

THOMAS L. TAYLOR

TED BENSON

TED BENSON

RICHARD STEINHEIMER

While SP's fleet of Alco passenger diesels traded their *Daylight* flash for grey and scarlet solemnity in the years before trade-in on new EMD power, the proud silver and red of Santa Fe's "warbonnet" was worn by Chico's favorite first class locomotives to the very end. Right at home on the *San Francisco Chief* to Chicago or scooting down to Bakersfield on one of the fast, frequent *Golden Gate* schedules, the big Santa Fe Alcos were equally at home on the containers and headend cars of *Fast Mail* Number 7, ready to depart Richmond on a long summer evening in the middle 1960s. By 1968, with SP's PAs gone and their own units on short time, Santa Fe saw fit to operate one last excursion for Bay Area fans (opposite) who'd long admired the grace and purity of the units belonging to the first Passenger Alco owner. In the hills east of Franklin Canyon near Muir station on March 3, 1968, ATSF Extra 67 East pauses for a photo run, doing so with a civility extending to the point of allowing one lucky photographer into the cab of PA 67 for a fresh look.

Tradition was always part of Santa Fe service, as reflected in Conductor H.C. Dewey's demeanor outside the Richmond station in the last days of pre-Amtrak service on ATSF's Valley Division. Dewey's beloved *Chief* was not on Amtrak's list for continuation after May 1, 1971, and come summer, Dewey would retire not in blue serge and brass but wearing the denim and twill of "freight service only."

JAMES E. BOYNTON

ROBERT SEARLE

Physical size of a railroad had little to do with the enormity of the corporate heart, as many railfans discovered in the formative years of their avocation. Hiking 14 miles roundtrip from his Piedmont home to the SP West Oakland roundhouse always provided Jimmy Boynton with good engine pictures, but going the extra mile to the modest Western Pacific roundhouse at the foot of Adeline Street resulted in real hands-on experience. Engineer Harry Davis welcomed the kid's Saturday visits, patiently explaining the intricacies of the machinery as they oiled around the 2-8-0 assigned WP's *Trevarno Local*, wrapping up the school session by allowing Jim to run the Hog from the roundhouse to the freight yard, make the air test, and then whistle for the SP interlocking before leaving town. By 1940, Boynton was working in WP engine service and attempting such exotica as night action photographs of WP's *Feather River Express* rattling the windows of the San Leandro station behind Ten-Wheeler 81.

Home from World War II, Christmas Day, 1946 sees Boynton watering 2-8-0 63 on the *Trevarno Local* at Niles, fellow railfan Bob Searle going along for a holiday outing to document Jim's avocation-turned-profession. Dinner that night was a can of pork and beans bummed off the cook of a work train at Livermore . . . spartan fare, but part and parcel of the adventure of growing up with trains.

THOMAS L. TAYLOR

Thirty years after young Jim Boynton haunted the WP Oakland roundhouse, another generation of photographers found the hospitable nature of the "Wobbly" little changed. In sharp contrast to nearby Espee facilities, one was welcome to make as many photographs as desired, recording *California Zephr* FP7s idling away the pre-dawn hours in the company of a GP40 that will follow the eastbound *CZ* down Third Street later that morning with the *Golden Gate Merchandise* in tow. Western Pacific was rightfully proud of the *Zephyr*'s Feather River routing, all the while hoping first-class customers wouldn't pay much heed to the second-class scenery punctuating train 18's path out of downtown Oakland.

TED BENSON

WILBUR WHITTAKER

RICHARD STEINHEIMER

WILBUR WHITTAKER

WILBUR WHITTAKER

AL HAIJ

The key to public transit in the East Bay of the '30s was the Key System, an amalgamation of several local streetcar companies providing a level of service unmatched in the days since the Key's untimely demise at the hands of National City Lines. Two years before the Bay Bridge opened, the Key ferry terminal in Oakland hosted a whole alphabet of travel options, including Sacramento Northern interurban schedules for the capital city and beyond. Competition for ridership came from SP's Red Electric lines, where a sunny spring Saturday in 1941 finds an Oakland-bound train passing SP diesel switcher 1009 at Parker Street in Berkeley. The island bedroom community of Alameda was served by the 4 Line of SP's Interurban Electric Railway, depicted on the opposite page, where a Red Car rolls off the Bay Bridge into San Francisco in January, 1939 when silver paint was fresh on signal boxes and overhead wire supports. By November, 1940, storm clouds gathered above the San Leandro Bay breakwater as an IER car enters Alameda, weather anticipating the end of Alameda suburban rail service the following January.

In the fruit salad days of the Key System's final hours, the bottom deck of the Bay Bridge was still reserved for buses, trucks and doubletrack as a city-bound train meets unit 170 in third-rail territory. Today, such meets transpire under the Bay mud in BART's doubletrack tube.

TED BENSON

ART ALTER/AL HAIJ COLLECTION

AL HAIJ

For little over 5 miles between Port Chicago and West Pittsburg, SN parallels both SP and Santa Fe and when schedules coincide, things get exciting fast. Rolling east of Nichols in 1938, SN train 2 (above left) overtakes SP 52, the motorman on the SN cars grabbing a couple more points on his controller and leaving SP 2468's nine heavyweights in his wake. Some 32 years later, an SN 44-ton diesel cabhopping east from the Port finds its 380 horses no match for the 1000HP Alco heading a Santa Fe local freight. "We were going downhill and he was still gaining on us!" SN hogger Ralph Waldren lamented to the photographer.

The Pacific Electric down south may have been the "world's greatest," but up north no one disputed Sacramento Northern's claim of "world's longest" interurban. In 1939 one ticket purchased 185 miles of electrifying transportation under catenary and beside third rail that crawled down city streets, flew down flat valley tangents, burrowed under the Oakland hills, sailed high over the $2 million bridge to San Francisco and paused to stretch the patron's legs for 15 minutes aboard *Ramon*, the only interurban train ferry in existence at the time. Spanning the Sacramento River west of Pittsburg from 1915 to 1954, *Ramon* provided dependable service for years after uniformed trainmen chatted on her deck and passengers from the *Comet* and *Meteor* took the air in SN's marine interlude.

By the summer of 1940, with the Treasure Island Exposition of 1939 closed and SN's passenger treasures fast fading, the 185 miles from the City to Chico were doomed. Car 1009 prepares to leave the Bay Bridge Terminal on August 26, 1940 with the last through train to Sacramento and beyond. After tonight, SN passenger service runs only to Pittsburg and then for but one more year.

ART ALTER/AL HAIJ COLLECTION

North of the Golden Gate the mountains come down to the sea, shadowy pockets beneath Mt. Tamalpais sheltering the big trees of Muir Woods and creating an extension of the Redwood Empire so close to the City as to become an ideal residential area. Railroads began serving the suburban transit needs of "marvelous Marin" in the 1870s, a growing network of narrow and standard-gauge lines ultimately becoming the Northwestern Pacific, and in 1902, under the aegis of predecessor North Shore, pioneering many of the concepts that spelled success for electrified suburban service worldwide. At first, converted steam coaches, many with open platforms and truss rod frames, provided accommodation. Public demand for improvements in the late 1920s led to the purchase of steel cars and rejuvenated depots like the classic stucco and tile building at Ross. When these photographs were made in late 1939 and early 1940, not even modern equipment and landscaped depot grounds could stop the inroads of rubber-tired transportation. Leaving the Manor terminal, NWP car 330 outweighed the Chevrolet waiting at the Point Reyes Road crossing, but the Chevy's flexibility and freedom rendered the electric coach a cost-inefficient dinosaur.

By the late 1950s, Northwestern Pacific steam power was all but gone and the Redwood Empire herald vanished, "Black Widow" freight diesels of parent Southern Pacific in firm control. The roads of Marin belonged to Ford and GM and the rails belonged to Cadillacs, as crews nicknamed the smooth-riding SD7s and SD9s dominating NWP's diesel detail. For school children in Novato, growing up with trains means a prized field trip on the friendly little *Redwood*, pausing on flag at the Novato depot one moody Monday morning in January 1957. Passenger service north of San Rafael was down to a thrice-weekly carding and the kids would have to go back to class on the bus, a travel option all NWP patrons would share once the 5327's two-car consist was discontinued south of Willits less than two years later.

ALL PHOTOS: TED BENSON

Tucked into a 1,390-foot Mendocino mountain valley, Willits marks the halfway point on the NWP mainline to Eureka, as well as the interchange with California Western's 40-mile trek to the ocean at Fort Bragg. Sporting a handsome depot built of the county's foremost legal export, Willits offers a superb show of hill-climbing railroad action despite the paucity of traffic on NWP's Eureka line in this summer of 1983. Cal Western cards two daily trips from Willits to Northspur, where the line trades summer-only passengers with an equal number of Fort Bragg-Northspur turns. Cresting the 3.5% climb over the Coast Range outside Summit tunnel with a low-nosed Alco RS-11 on the point, visiting railfans have difficulty deciding whether to aim their cameras at the majestic forest scenery or the attractive red Schenectady product powering the *Super Skunk*. By 1983, Alco diesel power in California is rarer than the steamers that hauled CWR tourists between 1965 and 1977.

South of Willits a midsummer's eve finds a Mendocino native perking his ears to the growing thunder of GM diesels, scampering off to safer ground as 12,250 horses come grumbling up the 2.2% north slope of Ridge Hill, the highest location on NWP. Seven Cadillacs thunder over the summit with a somewhat diminished load of perfumed forest products on the drawbar in the recession summer of 1981, slipping into dynamic braking for the 3% drop into Redwood Valley and Ukiah.

BOTH: KYLE BREHM

RICHARD STEINHEIMER

ALL PHOTOS: TED BENSON

In some ways, the history of Humboldt County railroading parallels the history embodied in the redwoods the rails were laid to cut and carry. Union Wharf & Plank Walk Company's 20 miles of primitive logging line around Eureka and Arcata, built in 1854, rank as the state's first rail miles, though often ignored because Union Wharf used four-legged horsepower in its earliest years. Today's Arcata & Mad River, whose ex-NWP caboose sees little use on the line from Blue Lake to Korblex, is a direct descendant of UW & PWC.

The mix of steam and diesel power dozing in The Pacific Lumber Company's Scotia enginehouse underscores the extent of TPL rail logging in the late '50s. TPL ran log trains until 1978, virtually undocumented by the line's isolation.

Better known to the public, but not through company advertising in later years, NWP's *Redwood* was still puttering down the Avenue of the Giants in 1969, Espee's Budd car having replaced a full trainset in 1959 after the *Redwood* was discontinued south of Willits in late 1958. The silver steel on the South Fork bridge replaced earlier spans lost to the raging Eel in the flood of 1964, and the relaxed pace of train 4 gave Conductor Charlie Coleman ample time to ponder the future of both his train and railroad. Amtrak ended NWP passenger service in 1971; 12 summers later, heavy winter storm damage in the Eel River Canyon and continued low lumber shipments led Espee to petition for abandonment north of Willits.

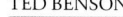

TED BENSON

Not all California redwoods are found north of San Francisco and not all SP surfside running is mainline, as the railroads of Santa Cruz County well illustrate. Logging brought narrow-gauge iron to the area in the 1870s and '80s and one hundred years later, the standard-gauge steel that remains holds on by the thinnest of margins; lumbering long ago was replaced by more earthy carloadings. Until 1982, the mountain grade of the old South Pacific Coast carried sand trains down from Olympia, where a steel cupola caboose carries the markers to end-of-track on a line that once went all the way to San Jose and Alameda. A few miles below the quarry, redwoods at aptly-named Big Trees provide clearance restrictions unlike any railroad in the nation. Along the coast north of Santa Cruz, cement shipments from the big mill at Davenport patiently follow a lone GP9 out of town on a chill February afternoon in 1969, the kind of day that makes big bowls of steaming clam chowder more welcome than gold.

At twilight, as fog reclaims the beaches south of Capitola, the *Santa Cruz Local* treads cautiously over the high bridge at Manresa, engineer Blair Kough carefully working throttle against air brakes to keep the sand and cement loads stretched before opening up his Geeps for the run at Ellicott Hill and the last miles into Watsonville Junction. The photographers pack the flash equipment and give thanks for the success of the venture, knowing without being told that the Santa Cruz Branch is living on borrowed time.

BRUCE MACGREGOR

Few who knew the *Coast Daylight* in steam would dispute its title of "most beautiful train in the world," and those appreciating the fine points of train operation easily agreed that the noontime meet of trains 98 and 99 on Santa Margarita Hill was the true highpoint of the day's journey from Los Angeles to the Bay. Teamed with a grimy 2-10-2 helper out of San Luis Obispo, *Daylight* 99 barks up the siding at Chorro, road engine 4448 keeping a clear stack on the 1.8% ascending grade as opposing *Daylight* 98 slides down the mainline behind another 4440 series 4-8-4, assured of having the east switch at Chorro cleared for a smooth rolling meet by a quick-reflexed trick dispatcher 246 miles away in San Francisco. Centralized Traffic Control wasn't common on SP in steam days, but there was nothing common about the *Coast Daylight*, or the line over the Santa Lucia Mountains.

BOTH: RICHARD STEINHEIMER

Steam power had come off the Coast Line's prime passenger runs in January 1955, banished to mail trains and commuter service in the final hours. Imagine Phelps' surprise, then, when he encountered the late running *Starlight* striding along the eucalyptus trees north of Burlingame behind 4-8-2 4376 on August 6, 1956, train 95's diesels having failed at Watsonville Junction on the trip from L.A. No diesels for the *Starlight* meant no diesels for the *Daylight* and Phelps stood fast, anticipating a reassigned GS engine on 98. Phelps was right, but the last engine he expected would be 4402, one of the pioneer GS1s!

BOTH: ALBERT C. PHELPS

RICHARD STEINHEIMER

PAUL LUKENS

A far more common chore for SP's venerable GS1s in the early '50s were blue collar commute runs like train 123, seen leaving South San Francisco (opposite) on an exceptionally misty morning, engine 4405 losing her footing on fog-slickened steel with twelve heavy "subs" on the drawbar. At least there are no more stops on the last nine miles into Third and Townsend. The early years of diesel on the *San Jose Passenger* find the afternoon "parade" lining up at Third Street in a majestic display of Fairbanks-Morse Trainmaster power, "Black Widow" paint glistening in the low sunlight. The big FMs were destined to become a Peninsula fixture over the next 20 years, almost as remarked upon during their 1974 retirement as the GS engines they had replaced.

Kid sisters to the 2,400HP Trainmasters were EMD's GP9s, locomotives kept off demanding rush hour schedules by their slower acceleration characteristics. One exception to the rule was train 126, the *Del Monte*, seen passing Redwood Junction behind a pair of "torpedo boat" Geeps in 1961. Considered a commute job on the Peninsula, the *Del Monte* dropped the suburban cars at San Jose before venturing on to Monterey for a gourmet dinner hour arrival, streamlined lounge and coach accomodations providing an extended cocktail party in genteel tradition. When Amtrak declined to pick up the service in 1971, the *Del Monte* vanished along with the honor of being the longest continuously run name train in the West.

RICHARD STEINHEIMER

San Francisco. Cable Cars.

For anyone who's left his heart in the City by the Bay and for those who've never been there, San Francisco and its rolling national historical landmarks are inseparable. Even if they *don't* climb halfway to the stars, a California Street car topping Nob Hill *can* do a fair job of eclipsing Bay Bridge support towers, and, considering the tourist dollars the cable lines rope in (12.5 million riders in 1981 alone), the decision to close the 10½ miles of cable track for a $58.2 million rebuilding was one the city fathers felt to be best for all. A few days before the September 1982 shutdown, "yardbird" Dave Rigor tapped out a jazzy requiem on a car bell as he hostled his charges outside the Washington Street barn, confident the somber "Cars Stop Here" sign in a nearby pavement applied only to the immediate future.

ALL PHOTOS—TED BENSON

While the cables were quiet, a willing Municipal Railway joined forces with the Chamber of Commerce to capitalize on one of the City's lesser-known rail attractions: the trolley lines. While new Light Rail Vehicles used the Market Street subway, Summer 1983 saw a historic trolley festival stage outside, with cars coming to San Francisco from all around the nation and world as well as the City's backyard. Accordingly, it was possible to see such incongruities as an ex-Muni "Iron Monster" meeting an LRV equipped for surface operation at the Castro Street terminus of the festival route—two generations of San Francisco street cars in one frame completely oblivious to the PCC era bridging the gap in trolley technology. As far as PCCs were concerned, the City had literally become a Valhalla for trolley fans in the 1970s, clinging to proven transit traditions long after the streamliners vanished from other "progressive" municipalities. The longevity of the green and cream PCCs paved the way for today's LRVs, further proof that much as things change in San Francisco, much remains the same.

ALL PHOTOS: RICHARD STEINHEIMER

As the tide flows through the Golden Gate, so must it ebb. Where once the steamer lanes were alive with ferries from five different railroads, the 1980s see just one rail marine operation left on the Bay. Considering its role as a technological pioneer, there's special irony that San Francisco's last rail vessels belong to Santa Fe.

It's true times have changed. Santa Fe's tugs and barges no longer meet on the gilded waters off Tiburon, shuttling carloadings from the Northwestern Pacific toward ATSF customers in the Midwest. Today, those lumber shipments leave the Redwood Empire in piggyback vans, getting out of Richmond in hours rather than days. One wonders if in the course of history the Santa Fe didn't win control of the NWP after all. Yet in this age of intermodal transportation, a few old habits linger on. 2,000 miles west of Topeka the dominant dynamics of a railroad at work are not turbocharged high-horsepower hood units but the low rumble of a marine power plant in tugboat "John R. Hayden," nosing car barges into slips at Point Richmond and China Basin. As foggy twilight engulfs the Bay Bridge, a rebuilt SW1200 grabs idler flats and begins anew the precise teamwork of man and machine required to spot steel-wheeled rolling stock on decks pitching with the rising swell.

JOHN E. SHAW

For the first transcontinental railroad there was one last mountain to cross between the Missouri River and the Golden Gate: Altamont.

The roundabout path from Sacramento to Oakland notwithstanding, opening of the Central Pacific through Altamont and Niles Canyon in the fall of 1869 completed the transcontinental rail link, eliminating a tedious river transfer from the capital. In later years, more direct lines to the Bay relegated Altamont to secondary status, though for railfans on both sides of the hill, Altamont remained common ground. With rails of both Western and Southern Pacific winding around the windswept, treeless hills, Altamont became a "poor man's Cajon," and a popular meeting place for those in search of relaxation as well as good photographs.

SP was always the preferred route for Altamont fans. When steam was long gone elsewhere on the system, cabforwards and double-slotted 4-8-4s still stormed out of Niles and Tracy to do battle with the one percent grade and eight degree curves on the hill, the drama lasting well into the sunset year of 1956, when John Shaw captured westbound timefreight 401 walking over the summit behind AC 4229. Transition in technology, underscored by the TV antenna atop the Altamont depot, fast undermined the line's importance, even in secondary usage. In 1956, that TV pulled in but three Bay Area stations. By 1981, if an Altamont depot still existed, the same TV would carry over 40 free channels plus several cable options. But by 1981, when Don Buchholz made his moody masterpiece of the East Pleasanton rock train rolling west in the rain near Sunol, SP operations over Altamont were sketchy at best. Two years later the line was broken for good, and before the '80s were half done, the rock train would be using the rails of neighbor WP, itself owned by Union Pacific through a merger that rendered the traditional transcontinental route of 1869 secondary on a grand scale.

GREAT VALLEY

AT FIRST GLANCE, the enormity of the land seems as numbing as its geographic similarity. The great Central Valley of California, 400 miles of unbroken plain from the Tehachapis to the Cascades, is billiard table flat and boring to many. Not the place one goes looking for a variety of rail photo subjects, right? Wrong! The geographic anonymity of the valley is deceiving, as are many first impressions. There are subtlties hidden behind that veil of seeming uniformity, so many that the closer one looks, the more one finds. To discover the nuances of the valley railroads is one of the great joys of growing up with trains in Northern California.

For starters, there's always Espee. Still an octopus of rail corridors and landholdings, the all-encompassing nature of Southern Pacific in the valley is just one of many stories. SP may be everywhere, but woven between are shortlines, former interurbans and mainline alternatives giving the old cephalopod a good run for the freight money in the 1980s. Case in point: Santa Fe.

A true symbol of free enterprise, built on the $5 and $10 subscriptions of valley farmers in a near-religious crusade against the crushing SP monopoly of the 1890s, the San Francisco & San Joaquin Valley "People's Road" between Stockton and Bakersfield came into the Santa Fe fold shortly after its completion in 1898, ATSF negotiating trackage rights over SP's Tehachapi line to reach the Mojave mainline connection for the East. Gerrymandered away from many established communities along the SP valley route, Santa Fe colonized the small towns it did serve direct and when necessary, created its own new habitations. Riverbank, 25 miles south of Stockton, arose from the need for a new division point in 1911, a village composed of roundhouse, depot, freight yard and little else. Sixty years after Riverbank's inception, with Amtrak about to temporarily remove Santa Fe's record-setting valley speedway from passenger applications, the eastbound *San Franciso Chief* eases out of the station siding as hotshot *NCX* slips down the main toward a quick crew change. New labor agreements will remove Riverbank's crew terminal status this summer of 1971 and 12 years later, the computer age will close Riverbank's freight agency, diesels long ago having made the local roundhouse a forgotten shell. As a railroad town, Riverbank is finished, but the solid food processing and manufacturing base good rail service has helped underwrite ensures the community's survival into a time when some may wonder why Riverbank has streets named "Atchison," "Topeka" and "Santa Fe."

TED BENSON

THOMAS L. TAYLOR

Living in close proximity to SP's mainline through Modesto did little to dampen the appreciation for Santa Fe held by two generations of local photographers. Spending his college years at Fresno State provided Tom Taylor with some fine opportunities to investigate the backwoods nature of Santa Fe's Valley Division at a time when many old traditions were in their twilight. The long dusk of June 1970 sees the eastbound *San Francisco Chief* rolling up Q Street toward the Fresno passenger station, four shiny F units leading the eight cars that were standard on Number 2 in her last full year of operation. The short, fast and frequent approach to manifest service coming on in the '70s increased Second District traffic density to the delight of shippers and railfans alike.

Before Santa Fe inaugurated the *San Francisco Chief* as the nation's newest (and last) transcontinental streamliner in 1954, one section of the *Grand Canyon Limited* turned north at Barstow to accommodate Bay Area Pullman patrons on the Southwest passage to Chicago. One train-length out of the Stockton station on a crisp winter afternoon in 1947, Al Rose catches the eastbound *Grand Canyon* rattling the diamonds at the SP-WP interlocking, Hudson 3454's engineer hooking her up for a fast sprint down the valley. A busy focal point for rail action in the port city, Stockton Tower continues to intrigue photographers today, despite the lack of such attractions as a *Grand Canyon Limited* behind high-wheeling 4-6-4s.

In sharp contrast to the stride of Number 24 is Santa Fe's *Oakdale Local*, strolling down the light rail of the erstwhile Oakdale & Western at Ladino, the only on-line station on the 6.5 miles between Riverbank and the Sierra Railroad connection. Not long after this warm afternoon of July 27, 1947, Consolidation 720 gave up the Oakdale District assignment to a zebra-striped 44-ton diesel.

BOTH: AL ROSE

GUY DUNSCOMB

TED BENSON

While Al Rose focused on everyday railroading Santa Fe-style, fellow Modestan Guy Dunscomb was making similar efforts on his hometown favorite Southern Pacific. Nine days before Rose captured the ATSF branch job at Ladino, Dunscomb prowls the mainline at Lathrop where *San Joaquin Daylight* 51 waits behind old reliable 4363, exchanging mail and cutting off through coaches for the connecting *Sacramento Daylight.* Entering its second summer of operation, train 53 made the River City run behind the 81" drivers of rebuilt Atlantic 3001 in the last regular assignment of four-driven steam on SP. While the shadows of dieselization grew long around Lathrop, the valley *Daylights* remained a steamy oasis until September 1956, Class A 4-4-2s and Mt 4-8-2s giving way to Pacifics and GS 4-8-4s in the final years. By 1969, when SP passenger service itself was in twilight, the through cars for Sacramento were dropped and riders for the capital made a cross-platform transfer on the unsheltered asphalt at Lathrop, where the engineer of Number 51's SDP45 casually surveys the action before rolling west for Oakland.

As Espee tuned up the valley corridor for increased competition in the deregulated 1980s, branchlines withered and fell away. In some cases, the last act was the most dramatic. On the morning of January 27, 1977, the entrenched fog of winter lifts to reveal Extra 3427 West crossing the Tuolumne River at Waterford, 142 stored PFE reefers leaving their temporary home near Hickman behind three GP9s in the last major train movement south of Oakdale. "Quite fascinating," Al Rose ruminated on the event, noting it had taken him 39 years to get a second chance at photographing rail activity on the magnificent structure. When evening mists descended, swirling around local power huddling close in the yard at Modesto, another chapter in the SP's valley fortunes was ready for the pens of the historians.

ALL PHOTOS: TED BENSON

GUY DUNSCOMB

BRUCE MACGREGOR

ALBERT C. PHELPS

"All roads lead to Roseville" local automobile dealers proclaim, but for Southern Pacific and its admirers, the revelation is nothing new. Hub of SP operations in Northern California since the seeming dawn of time, Roseville was an early "must see" for 16 year-old Jimmy Boynton and railfan photographer friend Guy Dunscomb, who made the portrait of "Shrimp" standing proud on the pilot of a brand-new 4159 on a 1937 excursion when the streamlined cab and big square tender of the AC-7's marked the beginning of a new generation of "Malley" power. In those days of youth for both photographers and their objects d'art, "excursion" connoted a fast ride on one of the many locals operating between the Bay Area and Roseville's many-columned depot, where on weekends and holidays one could obtain round-trip passage for the princely sum of $1.25!

On July 1, 1955, when Al Phelps got up early on a Friday morning to snare AC-10 4227 leaving Roseville for Gerber on Portland-bound manifest freight 492, the days of steam exhaust rolling over the station roof were numbered. Luckier than most Baldwin war babies of 1942, 4227 turned in 15 years of hard work before being vacated October 2, 1957, among the last two dozen of 195 4-8-8-2s that in concert with SP's streamlined *Daylight* engines gave the railroad a steam esthetic unmatched by any Western carrier.

A decade after train 492's Vesuvian departure on the East Valley line, an Alco entry in the second generation diesel dealer wars leaves Roseville for identical destinations with almost as much oil cloud to mark her going. Century 628 4857 digs down for most of the unit's 2,750HP on a June afternoon in 1965 when the 6-motor/4-motor superiority question was foremost in the minds of the "Big Three" domestic builders and Number Two diesel fuel was cheap. Sister C628 4871, an ex-demonstrator freshly relettered and numbered for SP but still in Alco gold and black waits to follow 4857's lead, an EMD F7 booster MU'd for a little extra tractive effort. After dark, another ex-demo unit idles in the Roseville shop area where Krauss-Maffei diesel-hydraulics like 9102 spent too much of their careers. A veteran of tonnage tests both in Austria and the US, the exotic 4,000HP cab is now confined to flatland service south and west of Roseville, fated for early retirement as part of an adventurous $9 million failure in SP diesel technology.

BOTH: RICHARD STEINHEIMER

RICHARD STEINHEIMER

RICHARD STEINHEIMER

Sacramento's credentials as a railroad town were established years before the Big Four, thanks to the Sacramento Valley Rail Road incorporating there in 1852 and opening to Folsom in 1856, five-feet-wide and steam all the way. Once local skeptics were convinced Central Pacific was more than a Dutch Flat swindle, the city's role in railroading was carved in stone. Andrew Stevens built his first locomotive there in 1873, establishing an eleven decade tradition carrying well into Diesel's second coming, where SP's Sacramento Locomotive Works turns out better-than-new rebuilds like SD45E 7465, posing for her producers in Spring, 1983. The presence of the California State Railroad Museum next to the SP shops underscores the preservation of the city's rail heritage, enlivened by local graduates like SP 0-6-0 1269 delighting tourists in the shadow of the capitol dome in May, 1982.

Not so well preserved is the local trolley heritage. Gone like the Western Hotel and its 50¢ rooms are City Lines cars turning the corner at 3rd. and K. Streets in 1947 as well as SN steeple cabs switching Central California Traction box motors along N. Street in 1937. Ironically, trolleys may run again in Sacramento, reinvented as "light rail systems," using part of the old SVRR Folsom line to keep the historic circle unbroken.

DON BUCHHOLZ

ART ALTER/AL HAIJ COLLECTION

AL HAIJ

AL HAIJ

HARRE DEMORO

TED BENSON

North of Sacramento, California's interurban heritage lives on, albeit increasingly fragmented. Diesels lettered "Sacramento Northern" ply isolated rails now belonging to Union Pacific, and precedessor Northern Electric's initials are an integral part of the bridgework that carries SN switch crews across the Feather River between Marysville and Yuba City. Back in 1946, when nickel candy bars still cost 5¢, Al Haij stopped by Chico, NE's birthplace, to spend his candy money for a ride on Birney car 60, a local tradition that vanished the following year along with the state's last nickel fares and Birney service. When Western Pacific F3 cab unit 803A began her *California Zephyr* career in 1949, vista dome passengers in Marysville were alarmed to find a 1200 volt copper power line an arm's reach overhead, a condition existing until 1965 when a pair of used WP SW1s pulled the breaker on SN's last island of electricity.

WILBUR WHITTAKER

TED BENSON

TED BENSON

South of Sacramento, interurban customers could take the Central California Traction to Lodi and Stockton, continuing on to Modesto via Tidewater Southern as late as 1932. Electric freight engines of the WP subsidiary lasted into 1948, thanks to a Modesto franchise restriction forbidding steam power on city streets, creating sights like motor 100 towing Tidewater Tenwheeler 1 and a four-car freight out of the Modesto depot in August 1939. In fall, numerous harvest extras filled the TS with WP locomotives and passengers could purchase caboose tickets until 1957. By 1967, as engineer Sy Black napped in the cab of 44-tonner 735 awaiting a meet at Modesto's Aurora siding, growing TS tonnage slated the little GE diesel for retirement, erasing forever the sleepy backwoods trolley image. Today, power from new owner UP propels growing numbers of general freight and unit grain trains between Stockton and Turlock, delighting young fans like Amy and Jessica Benson who share their father's joy of growing up with the Tidewater as the family backyard railroad.

While controlled in thirds by SP, Santa Fe and Western Pacific, which by 1984 means UP and the nation's newest merger partners, CCT maintains a fiery red (and white-striped) independence. Sacramento-bound with 44 cars of export coke and 3 tanks of coconut oil, GP18 1795 and GP7 70 cross the Dry Creek trestle north of Lodi in April 1982. Bulk commodities have not been the Traction Company's forte, unfortunately, and the line's redundant route is cause for concern in the transitional times ahead.

DAVE STANLEY

The gold country southeast of Sacramento is home for a rich collection of branches and shortlines, perhaps none better known than the fabled Sierra Railroad, whose noted Rogers 4-6-0 Number Three has appeared in enough miles of 35 millimeter celluloid to rate her her own star on Hollywood Blvd. Shuffling up to the Warnerville water stop immortalized by *High Noon* (past a new tank built for *Nickelodeon*), Sierra 3 presents a timeless tableau, complete with young Britton Coffer cavorting around the tank frame in the manner of youthful railfans of old. Only those closest to the action can date the scene—December 8, 1982.

The least-likely locomotive for a lumber-hauling mountain railroad had to be General Electric's 380HP 44-tonner. California foothill lines went for the units in a big way, light rail and spindly trestlework winning out over lack of tractive effort. Amador Central 8 replaced steam power between Ione and Martell in 1945, grinding out a 25-year career on the undulating AC profile before bowing to Baldwin replacement power in 1970. Heroically-named Camino, Placerville & Lake Tahoe never got near the lake, but held on to an equally-elderly GE until 1971, when CP&LT's "second generation" was ushered in by a used 44-tonner built in February, 1941. Camino's new engine leaves the SP interchange at Placerville on a wet April Monday in 1972, traction motors outshouting prime movers on the 3% grade. When the old Burlington Route claimed "Everywhere West," they meant business!

ALL PHOTOS—TED BENSON

RICHARD STEINHEIMER/DE GOLYER LIBRARY

That steam locomotives ran anywhere of consequence in 1958 was cause enough for celebration. When the locomotives were 3-foot-gauge Shays of the West Side Lumber Company, railfans mounted pilgrimmages to the Tuolumne hills, filling the day with dusty auto rides into forbidding Sierra canyons and filling the night with bursts of light, all in one last campaign to document what had once been commonplace everywhere. Geared engines hauled forests to sawmills by the trainload and now stood imperiled by improved truck roads into high timber stands. Bundled against the nip of early fall, Bob Hale, Warren Marcus and Jack Lucey capture the passing of West Side 10 and engineer Shorty Maddox, empty log flats rattling back to the woods in the hours before dawn. Come October 28, 1960, Maddox and his treasured Ten Spot would bring the last load of rail-hauled logs through the Tuolumne mill gate and the steamless Sierra nights would be flash-filled no more.

ART ALTER/AL HAIJ COLLECTION

Last runs have always been a part of growing up with trains.

Economics overrule emotion and probably always will.

Some goodbyes were notable: for the beers washing away NWP's last ferry and electric rail service to Marin, the tears at the demise of the blueblooded Yosemite Valley, the jeers at Sierra's multiplicity of "farewell" steam excursions, and the fears that the end of WP's *California Zephyr* was just the beginning of worse things to come.

Some goodbyes were quiet, like the unheralded scrapping of the San Joaquin & Eastern in the hills above Fresno, TenWheeler 201 winding out of the chaparral with diminishing rail ahead and empty ties behind in July, 1935. Sometimes the last light of day on such seemingly-imperturbable lines like SP's Kentucky House branch out of Lodi holds more than the eye realizes. The SD9s following the canyon of the Calaveras River into the autumnal hills above Valley Spring wouldn't last forever, but the big cement mill at "K-House" was good for decades . . . or so it seemed in November, 1974. Today the mill is closed and the line stores unwanted boxcars, all victims of the beginning of basic change in a production-oriented economy. Where twilight falls tomorrow no mortal can know.

THE MOUNTAINS

THE SP FLANGER POWER riding the turntable at Dunsmuir on a snowy night in the Sacramento River Canyon illustrates the extreme contrast between mountain railroading in Northern California and the railroading practiced elsewhere in the state.

Forget your tangent track, and billiard table grade profiles. Forget, too, the mild winters along the shores of the Pacific Ocean. Forget also those grand miles-away desert scenes; probably 100 pine trees will be in the way.

Make no mistake, the great mountain ranges that cut off the Great Valley from Oregon and Nevada are the equal of anything you'll find in the lower 48 states. The SP mainline ties above Truckee are touched by frost nearly every morning in the year, and the more than 400-inch snowfall average at the top of Donner Pass has been a world class proving ground for management ever since Charlie Crocker fought the Sierra Nevada Mountains to a stand-still with his Chinese and Irish workforces.

Scores of small railroads and branchlines once battled the great ranges of the Cascades and the Sierra. Very probably, thousands of miles of temporary logging lines were laid in these canyons before the timber ran out and Forest Service practices favored truck logging. Though not as numerous as in Oregon and Washington, the logging lines of Northern California perhaps made up for it in uniqueness.

At least one logging line, Long-Bell near Mt. Shasta, had its own homemade rotary snowplow. The amazing Red River Lumber Company of Westwood also logged in winter but used borrowed SP rotaries. However, they did buy a 600 horsepower Alco-GE-Ingersoll-Rand diesel electric in 1926, the first diesel road power on the Pacific Coast. Even more incredible, the Red River hauled logs on a 1500-volt electrified district, basically following the route of today's Almanor Railroad.

Many people can still remember when the SP branch still hauled passengers and private railroad cars right down to the edge of the deep blue waters of Lake Tahoe.

Not everything is just history with small railroads in these mountains. The Quincy Railroad, the Camino, Placerville and Lake Tahoe Railroad, the McCloud River Railroad, the Yreka Western Railroad and the Almanor Railroad still climb hills with steel wheels on steel rails.

Amtrak's *California Zephyr* provides an exciting view of SP's big time railroading in the Sierra. Probably most surprised by this ride are the people who have already "seen the Sierra" from their cars on Interstate 80. The route Theodore P. Judah laid out follows a continuous ridge all the way to the summit, affording views of incredible canyons in the watersheds of the American and Yuba Rivers. If you don't mind a few zombied-out companions, the *Reno Fun Train* also heads west over The Hill from Sparks on Sunday mornings in winter.

Turn the page and experience the wonderful gift of photographs . . . from people who grew up with these mountains.

RICHARD STEINHEIMER / DE GOLYER LIBRARY

ALBERT C. PHELPS PHOTOS

The 1940s and 1950s are greatly illuminated by the camera work of a pair of SP employees who show us what it takes to do good photographs in the upper Sacramento River Canyon. For Albert C. Phelps and Wilbur C. Whittaker, Friday nights often meant getting home early from work and jumping aboard the *Klamath* mail train for the all-night ride to Dunsmuir. Then a dawn departure up the right-of-way for the 15-mile walk to the town of Mount Shasta. A true dynamic duo, they occasionally make the roundtrip in a day.

A wonderful image from the fall of 1951 shows the westbound *Klamath* easing down the 2% grade at Cantara siding behind GS-2 #4410, first SP streamlined 4-8-4.

Phelps also captures cab-forward helper #4198 returning light to Dunsmuir past his pal.

The glory and thunder of 1-632 blasting up the canyon near Shasta Springs is caught by Whittaker's camera. In the far distance, beyond cab-forward # 4291, his hiking partner waits for a repeat performance by the rear end helpers.

WILBUR C. WHITTAKER

It is August of 1951, and manifest 2-632 has struggled up the grade from Dunsmuir only to stall in front of Phelps's lens. Foaming of the boiler, and having to build pressure again in helper #4133, has stalled 2-10-2 #3689 and cab-forward #4151 at the worst spot in the canyon . . . right on 10 degree Cantara Loop. Without the benefit of today's train radio, it is nearly 30 minutes before cars can be set out and the train can start moving again.

The flow of railroading in the canyon has been upset, with the final result being the *Shasta Daylight* dropping down the grade a full 40 minutes late. The beautiful E7 locomotives and the red and orange *Shasta Daylight* chair cars . . . frozen on film for all time by Phelps's camera.

BOTH PHOTOS: ALBERT C. PHELPS

ALBERT C. PHELPS

The steep bluff to which the rails cling above Cantara Loop is the location for this Phelps view of helper #4131 returning to Dunsmuir after helping a train to Black Butte or Grass Lake. It is in the summer of 1949—the beginning of the *Cold War*—prompting an angry trainman to lean from the cab to loudly encourage the "Commie" photographer to hit the trail.

The days of Phelps and Whittaker in the Canyon will start to draw to a close as sections of 632 start climbing the bluff with new 1500 horsepower SD7 locomotives. Today's trains still climb the bluff to escape the Canyon, but the locomotives have 3600 horsepower in each carbody, and even the trailing refrigerator cars have diesel power plants.

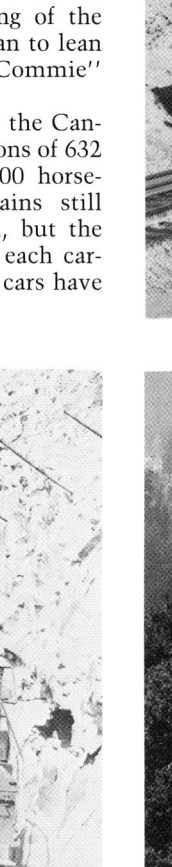

HAROLD ESTUDILLO

DICK DORN

RICHARD STEINHEIMER PHOTOS/DEGOLYER LIBRARY

The arrival of diesels to the Shasta Route in the early 1950s frees big steam power for use on the Modoc line, which slices south from Klamath Falls across the northeastern tip of California. We see the engineer of 2-551 taking a second try at the eastbound 1% grade of Viewland Hill north of Wendel. His head brakeman waits to flag the lonely US 395 crossing. Then under a mighty pillar of oil smoke, #4159 finally storms over the crossing fast enough to make the summit.

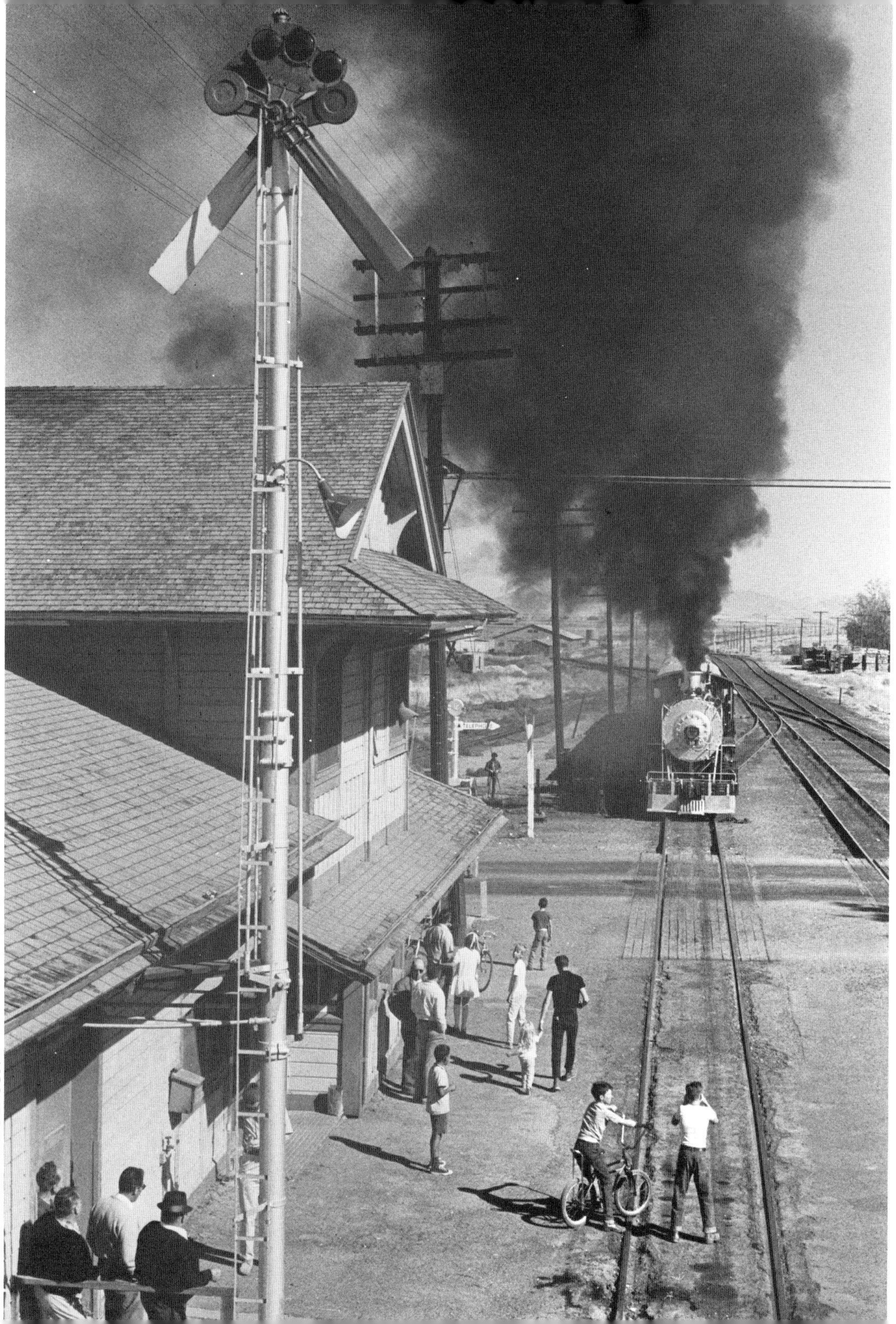

TED BENSON

DICK DORN

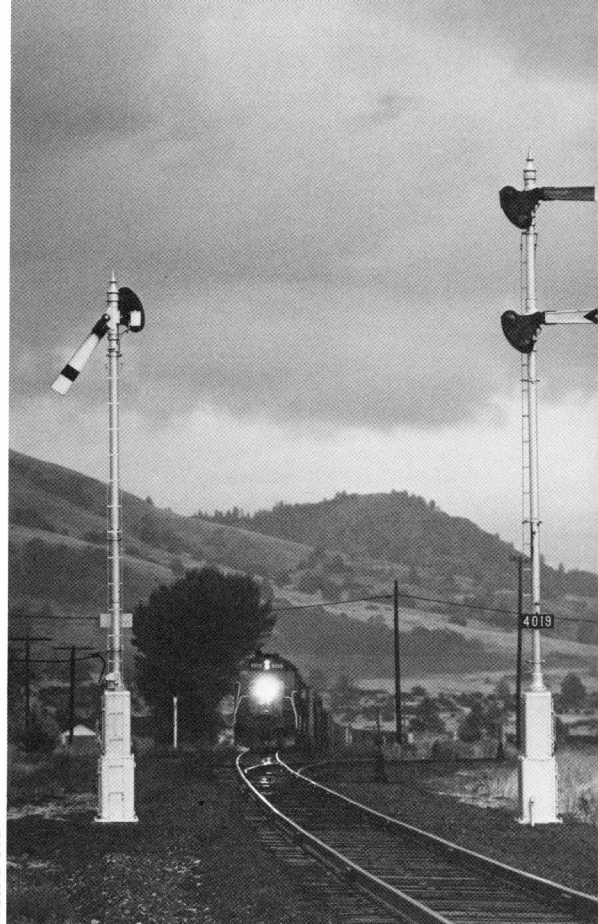

A full 800 miles north of Los Angeles, the little Yreka Western Railroad closes out its steam era on October 11, 1970. To the full appreciation of the local kids who have ridden down to the depot to see the action, Mikado #19 makes a stirring entrance into the SP Siskiyou line junction at Montague.

Several years later an eastbound SP train sets the semaphores to ''stop,'' leaving the little lumber town of Hilt just a mile before it hits the Oregon border on the ascent of Siskiyou summit.

The fantastic 1981 tour of SP #4449 (right) brings steam back to the Shasta Route. We see the beautiful 4-8-4 leaving the summit at Grass Lake, *sans* helpers, for the quick 40-mile descent to Dorris and the Oregon line. For thousands of fans, the tour was best described as ''unbelievable.''

JEFF BROUWS

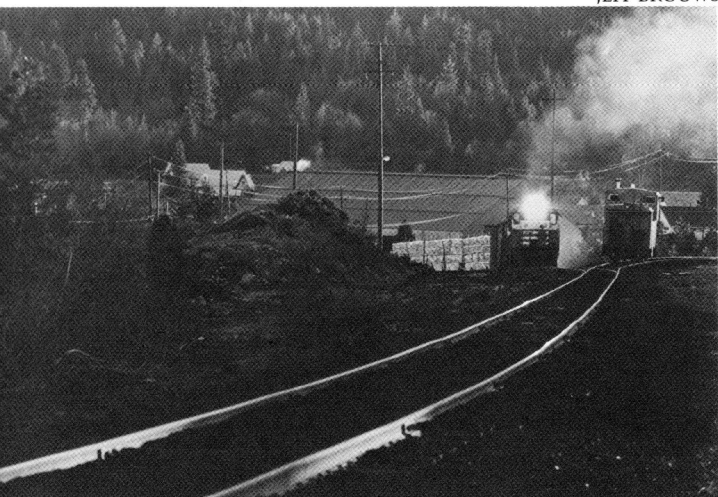

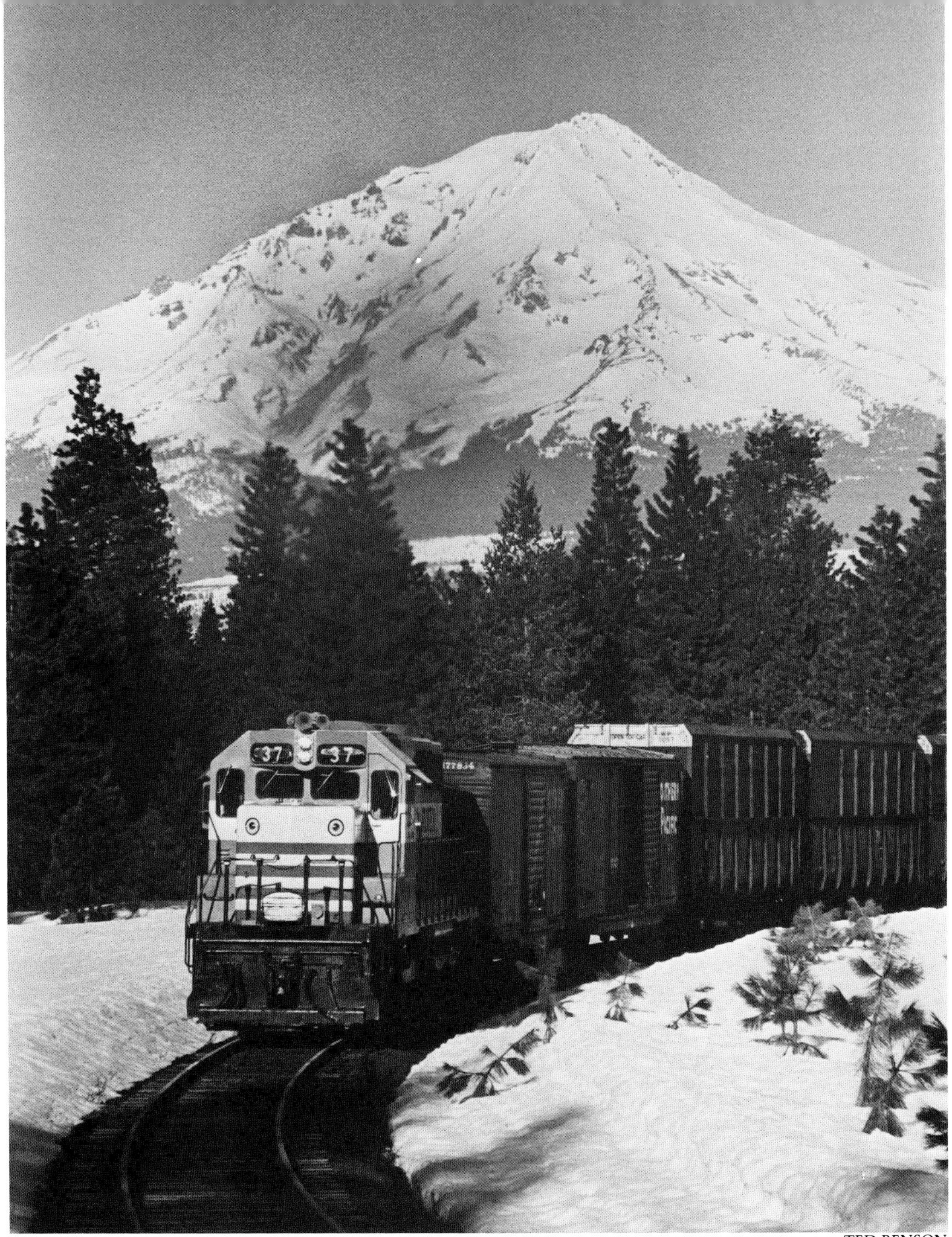

TED BENSON

The McCloud River Railroad, which still serves the sparsely populated Cascade wilderness east of the SP junction at Mount Shasta City, is certainly the archetype of Northern California mountain shortlines. The road operates from its headquarters at McCloud, east to a junction with the BN at Lookout, and south to forest products plants at Burney. Today, we see the Burney job heading south beneath the *massif* of Mount Shasta with a train of empties, the SD38 power rolling through a countryside of giant pines, rivers and mountains suitable for any Hollywood movie.

The camera of Jeff Brouws captures the outbound loads being gathered at McCloud in the Cascade twilight, before the train is assembled for the climb up the steep switchbacked grade to the SP at Mount Shasta.

TED BENSON

A real mountain favorite . . . McCloud #25 shows its stuff at Bartle in 1975 on its last trip before restoration at McCloud in 1982. The beefy little 2-6-2, one of the few surviving rod engines from the forests of Northern California, still serves the railroad on special occasions.

The Keddie station stop of the eastbound *Feather River Express* in the 1940s is captured in masterful detail by the camera of Guy Dunscomb, one of the great fans of the Western Pacific Railroad. While the engineer oils the valve gear of the 4-6-0, the fireman takes water, and passengers on the far side of the train stretch their legs and sniff pure mountain air temporarily untainted by the somewhat sulphurous output of the #77. Passengers continuing east beyond Portola will detrain there to wait for the more grand early morning arrival of the *Exposition Flyer*.

A leisurely pace of railroad activity at Keddie in May of 1938 is suggested by this classic Dunscomb view of motive power for a "Four Bagger" lined up outside the roundhouse. Behind "Baby Mallets" #202 and 204 are two more 2-6-6-2's, comprising the road engine and three helpers for the next freight train up the Inside Gateway, or High Line, to Bieber. Western Pacific practice is to space the helpers evenly through the train, allowing these powerful "Babies" to move 4500 tons together up the 2.2% ruling grade to Lake Almanor.

WILBUR C. WHITTAKER

Number 259 is anything but a "Baby" Mallet as she leads this westbound freight across Keddie wye in the 1940s. Before the ten powerful 2-8-8-2's of this class were ordered, crews were polled to see if they favored a cab-forward configuration. Probably influenced by the frequent rockslides and collisions on the non-signaled single track, they asked for a normal cab position. The one million pounds plus locomotive is capable of taking 70-car reefer blocks up the Feather River Canyon's 1% grade at about 20 miles an hour. The leg of the wye leading off to the left is the beginning of the 112-mile High Line to Bieber.

The Western Pacific has always attracted fans, such as this car trip in May 1947, by (from left) Dudley Thickens, Albert Phelps, Doug Richter, and Guy Dunscomb. After the self-portrait, Dunscomb shoots the dramatic sky and block signal at Chilcoot, and then Richter standing with his camera with the beautiful Sierra Valley in the distance.

GUY DUNSCOMB PHOTOS

RICHARD STEINHEIMER

That railroad action has always been interesting along the Feather River Route can be guessed by the variety of motive power to be found in these mountains. In later years, you could find WP F-units heading eastward from Portola in winter, past the frozen PFE icing dock. An earlier fan trip found one of the six WP 4-8-4s stopped at the Keddie roundhouse. Down at Quincy Junction, one can always watch the little 44-tonner of the Quincy Railroad doing its thing with woodchip cars.

WILBUR C. WHITTAKER

TED BENSON

WILBUR WHITTAKER

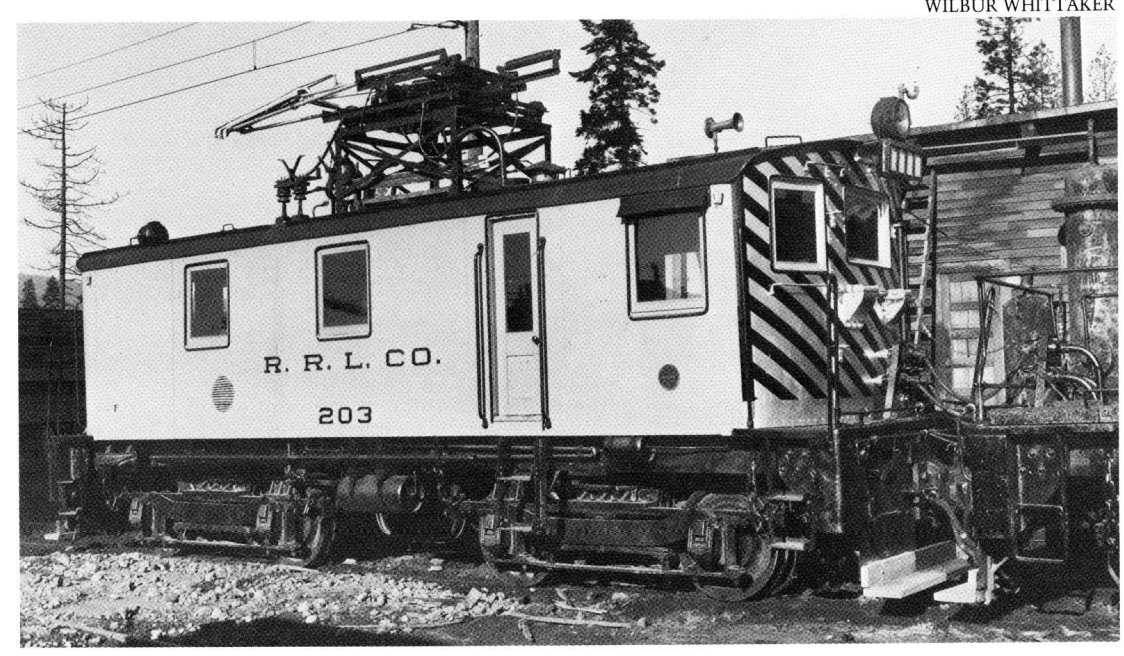

At Westwood, on the WP's High Line, there are the 1500 volt electric logging locomotives of the Red River Lumber Company to look out for. Motor #203 derives her unique styling courtesy of rebuilding after a wreck. Modern to the limit, Red River bought the first diesel electric road engine on the Pacific Coast in 1926—from Alco-GE—Ingersoll-Rand. At Hawley, the Feather River Lumber Company dashes across the WP mainline headed for its reload point. Today, the little 2-6-6-2 is preserved at Castro Point by the Pacific Locomotive Association.

RICHARD STEINHEIMER/DE GOLYER LIBRARY

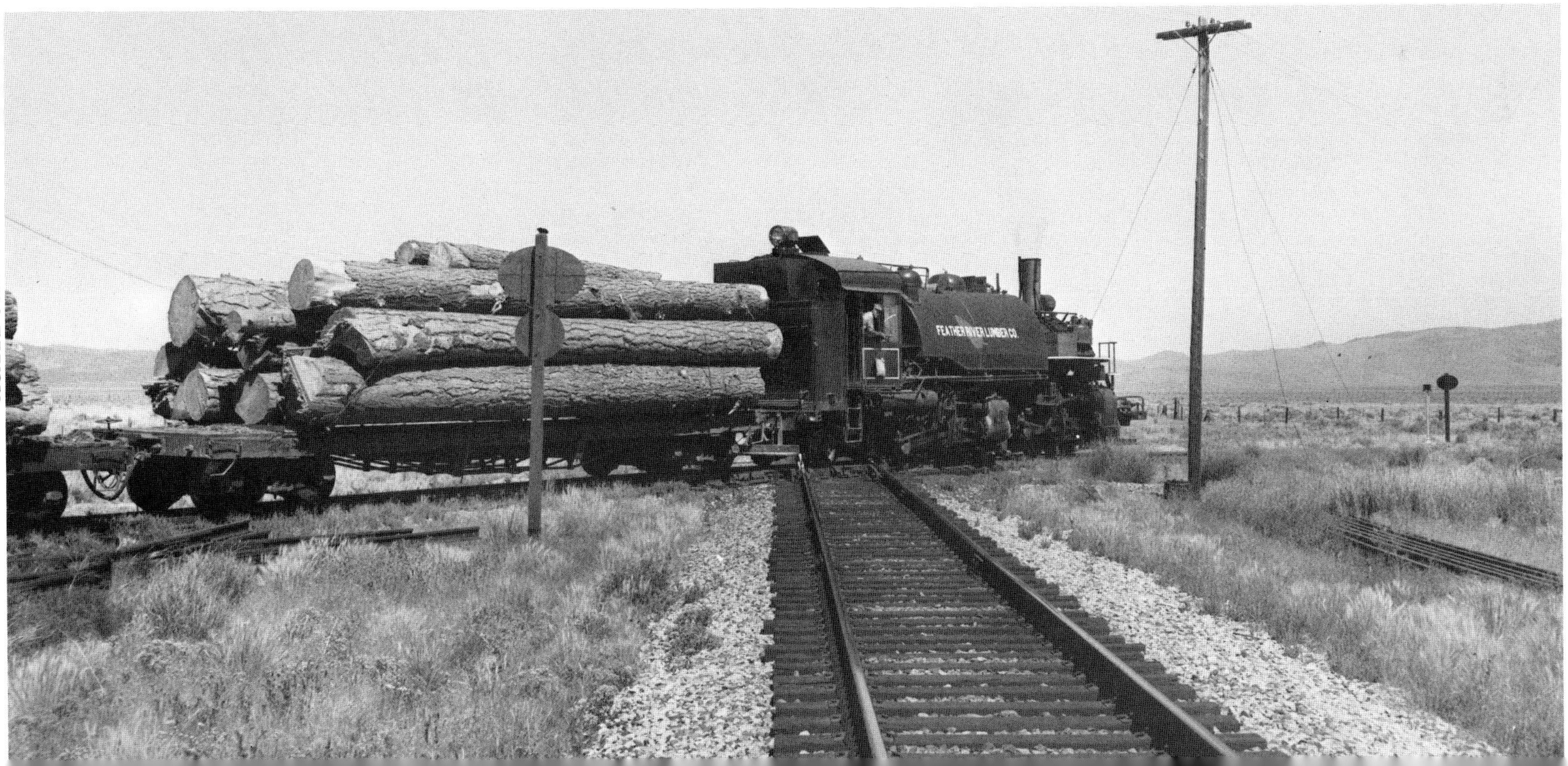

TED BENSON

DICK DORN

A quarter-century after Dunscomb, Richter, Phelps and Thickens brave the backroads above Keddie, the next generation of Western Pacific devotees heads into the Plumas woods. At Greenville on a December Sunday, the weather is anything but inviting as the first section of train 54 takes a run at the 2.2% west of the depot, four chugging GEs already working hard on the 1% ascending. Doubtless the local trainmaster would frown at the mixed green and white flags fluttering over the 758's cab. Inside Greenville station, Dick Dorn thaws out in front of the heater adjoining a safe that still wears the gold leaf of the original Western Pacific Railway, while wife Chris peruses Saturday's newspaper, patiently passing time until Second 54 blows by on the climb up to Almanor.

TWO PHOTOS—TED BENSON

Two decades after sharing steamed pork and beans with Bob Searle on the *Trevarno Local*, Jim Boynton holds down engineer's seniority and still shares his day's work with a few selected passengers. Voice booming over the roar of six F7s heading up the eastbound *Expediter*, Boynton explains High Line operations to Tom Taylor while keeping the sanding valve down in deference to the hill above Greenville. For two skinny kids from Guy Dunscomb's backyard, the June 1968 Bieber trip begins a friendship lasting long after the covered wagons are gone from the Inside Gateway. Five winters later, that bond brings the photographer back to Keddie Wye, where High Line hood units in green pause for the passage of a mainline train before rolling west toward Oroville.

TED BENSON

The High Line pool train erupting from a tunnel east of Virgilia with mixed Alco and EMD power is one of the memorable images arising from the anything-but-dull operations of the Western Pacific in the Feather River Canyon. In just a few years the Alcos will be gone, and the Union Pacific presence will greatly increase.

The shadowy meeting of trains at Camp Rogers siding deep in the canyon is another visual memory to be treasured. Here the Geneva steel train, at left, is waiting in the hole for an eastbound hotshot.

Canyon fog diffuses the headlight of BN-139 negotiating the "slot" below Pulga on May 1, 1978 as a new day dawns for WP. Stepping off the pool train a few hours earlier, Jim Boynton ended 20 years on the High Line, closing the book on Keddie as a crew terminal. Later-day railroaders work straight through from Oroville to Bieber while Boynton runs out his last miles east of Portola. Shortly after sunrise on August 22, 1981, a new day dawns for the kid who grew up with trains, leaving Hawley westbound for retirement after 40 years of WP engine service. For Jim Boynton's beloved "Wobbly," only 16 months of independence remain. December 22, 1982 consummates WP's merger into Union Pacific, realizing the Feather River Route's grand transcontinental designs as envisioned by Arthur Keddie and George Gould eight decades before.

ALL PHOTOS: TED BENSON

The popular image of WP as everybody's favorite underdog is vanishing as fast as the melting April snow. Seventy-five cars of Midwestern grain wind around Williams Loop in the spring of 1982, with UP rolling stock front and rear, foretelling the look of the future in the canyons of the Rio de las Plumas.

ALBERT C. PHELPS

Albert Phelps climbs to a hilltop near Cape Horn, above Colfax, on June 23, 1941, to shoot his favorite picture . . . the last eastbound run of the *Forty-niner*. The eight car all-Pullman extra fare train is barely crawling up the hill, despite the best efforts of the 4-8-2 and the 2-8-0 added at Colfax. We can expect the little Consolidation to continue on to the summit today, instead of making its usual turn at Emigrant Gap. The *Forty-niner* began service in the summer of 1937, running five times a month alternately with the *City of San Francisco*—on about an eight hour slower schedule. In three days, a second *City* set will go into service to replace this rare bird of a train.

The cab-forward and the 2-8-0 helper pounding up the Sierra Nevada grade through Gold Run in 1946 is one of the dramatic expressions of mainline mountain railroading on SP's Donner Pass. In a moment, this troop train section of the *San Francisco Overland Limited*, carrying green flags for another section, will enter The Hill's automatic train control territory. Electronics for the cab signalling system are carried in the box on the pilot of the Consolidation. Theodore P. Judah surveyed the route, and four Sacramento shopkeepers got the rails of the Central Pacific to the summit of the Sierra in 1867, only 18 years after the end of Mexican rule in California.

88

WILBUR C. WHITTAKER

The open front coupler hatch on #6011 with train 26 at Reno suggests a stormy helper-assisted passage for the mail train over Donner Pass. The E2 lead unit is the fomer SF-1 of the 1937 *City of San Francisco*. In later years it will be rebuilt and renumbered as the 6017—the *Queen Mary* to railroad fans.

Even more rare is the first *City of San Francisco* pictured in June 1936, by a young Western Union delivery boy at Auburn. Albert C. Phelps has hung around the depot to catch the first westbound test run of the new automotively-styled Streamliner, boasting a total of 2400 horsepower in its two power units. Phelps will continue his SP career in a variety of jobs at Auburn and Roseville before retiring in 1977.

ALBERT C. PHELPS

RAILWAY NEGATIVE EXCHANGE

A new chanting sound came to the snowsheds of Donner Pass in the late 1940s with the arrival of the first F7 freight diesels. For Albert Phelps and Ken Yeo, it meant getting out on the road to take all the pictures they could. On this helper trip to Norden, the ex-El Paso and Southwestern 4-8-2 they rode waits outside the Norden sheds for one of the new diesels to couple on behind for the trip right back to Roseville. The EMD units were not yet equipped with the automatic train control cab signals required between Truckee and Gold Run.

RICHARD STEINHEIMER PHOTOS/DEGOLYER LIBRARY

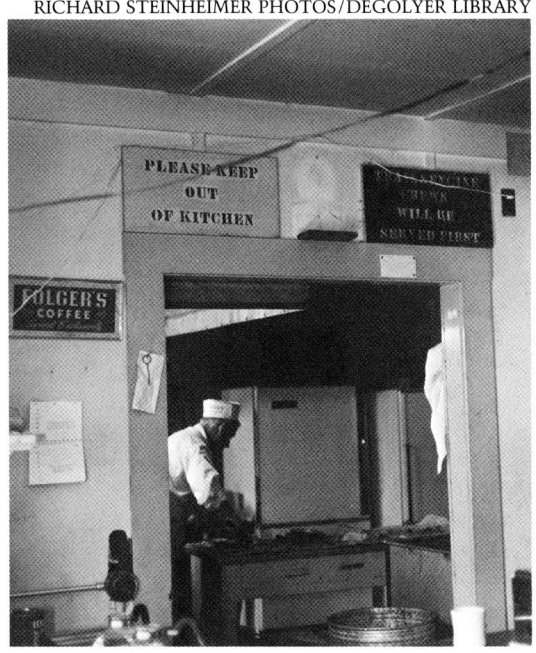

A memorable and seemingly permanent fixture maintained for employees at Norden, before it burned down, is the "Chinaman's" cookshack. What more could railroad fans want? It combined difficult access through a hole in the snow, with lots of non-elegant dining, beneath a sign which warns you that train and engine crews will be served first!

By 1966 the old cookshack is gone, and the throaty new voices in the snowsheds are those of brand new 3000 horsepower SD40 locomotives, inheritors of 100 years of Central Pacific history on this hill.

92

CLINT NESTELL

DICK DORN

Today, we find most of the Donner Pass snowsheds gone, or rebuilt in cement. Powerful electric rotary plows like the MW 211 clearing the way for Amtrak at Soda Springs, are not required some winters with lesser snowfalls. On another day, at the same location, we see the westbound Amtrak passenger train whisking its riders quickly and comfortably over the mountains which were so brutal to the earliest immigrants.

Overlooking Donner Lake, a westbound freight train emerges from cement-covered tunnel 7, near the top of the grade, and the start of the 85-mile winding descent to the floor of the Great Valley at Roseville.

RICHARD STEINHEIMER

WILBUR C. WHITTAKER

ALBERT C. PHELPS

ALBERT C. PHELPS

The SP mainline is not the only action in the Sierra, a region once so populated with railroads as to boggle our aerobic computerized minds. To illustrate: we can admire this daily mixed train of the three-foot gauge Nevada County Narrow Gauge Railroad proceeding gloriously over Cedar Kress summit in January 1939, on its 21-mile journey from the SP connection at Colfax to the mining town of Nevada City. The adjacent highway, already cleared of snow at taxpayer's expense, will completely supplant this 53-year-old Mother Lode institution in just three years.

Before World War II, the Pacific Portland Cement Company (left) operates this spectacular limestone-hauling steam railroad from Auburn down into the deep American River Canyon, complete with trestles and even a switchback near the summit.

North of Camino, the Michigan-California Lumber Company freight car cableway across the south fork of the American River provided a hair-raising thrill for fans adventurous enough to want to see the woods operation.

COLOR FAVORITES

RICHARD STEINHEIMER

Wouldn't it be fun to go back in time .. to be able to see the Dunsmuir roundhouse full of steam again, and feel the excitement of such a beautiful Cascades morning.

On the SP's Coast Line, cab-forward #4224 moves to cut in a rear end helper at Santa Margarita for the short 2.2% climb of Cuesta Grade.

Mission Bay roundhouse (above) in San Francisco sees #2468 getting her train indicators changed for a Peninsula commute run to San Jose. Thirty years later, three SP 4–6–2's are being restored by Bay Area fan groups.

The engine (opposite) everyone will love, #4449, moves out from between sisters 4448 and 4451 at Mission Bay to take the advance section of the *Coast Merchandise East* on its 470-mile flight to Los Angeles.

RICHARD STEINHEIMER PHOTOS

RICHARD STEINHEIMER

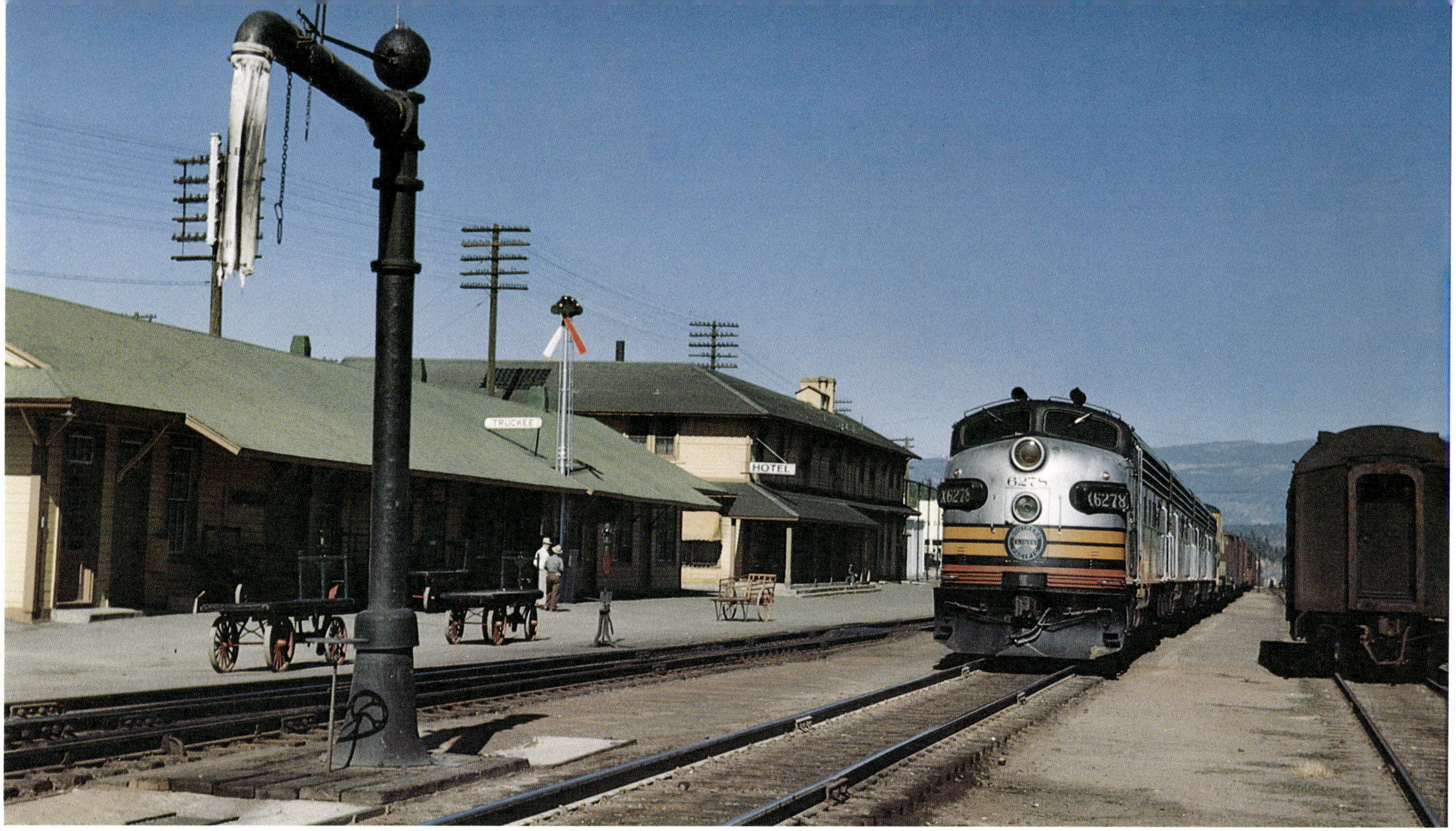

PAUL LUKENS

The diesel age which overtook Northern California put so many F-units on the Western Pacific that some fans considered them boring. By March 1980 (left) they were rare enough to encourage Don Buchholz to tough it out for hours to catch four of the units bringing a San Jose Turn to the summit at Altamont. Number 913 wears its old paint scheme preparatory to its donation to the California State Railroad Museum.

Thirty years earlier (above) the SP Hotel and other artifacts of the steam age were being obsoleted by brand new four-unit sets like #6278 as the diesel age came to Truckee.

Ten years later (right) at Sacramento, SP still relies on Alco PA power for the *San Francisco Overland*, getting ready to pull out for a stormy crossing of Donner Pass.

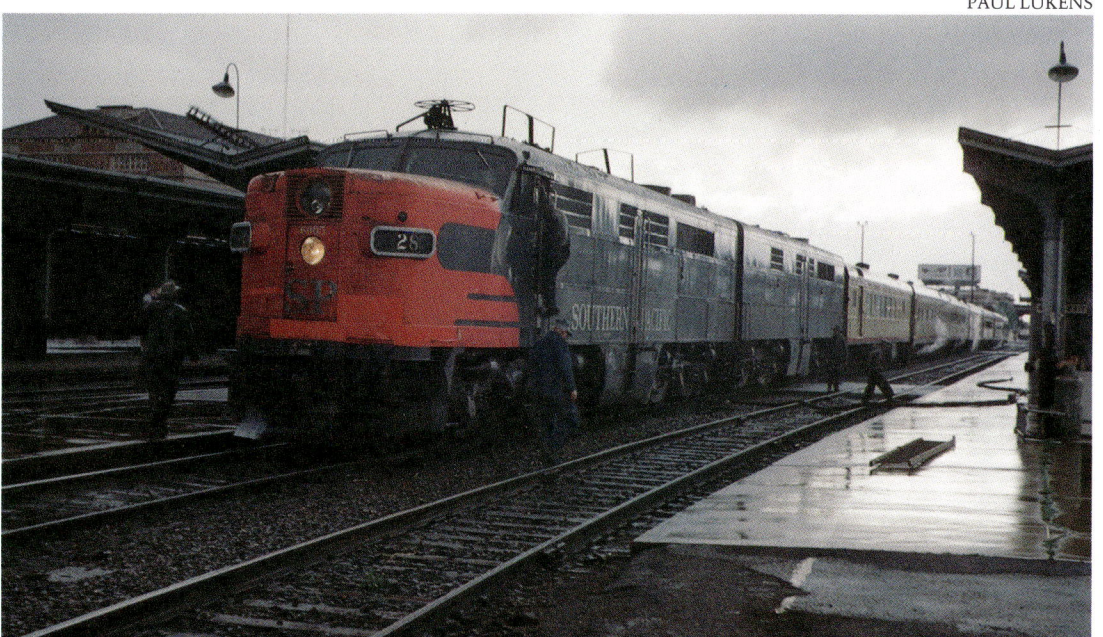

RICHARD STEINHEIMER

DON BUCHHOLZ

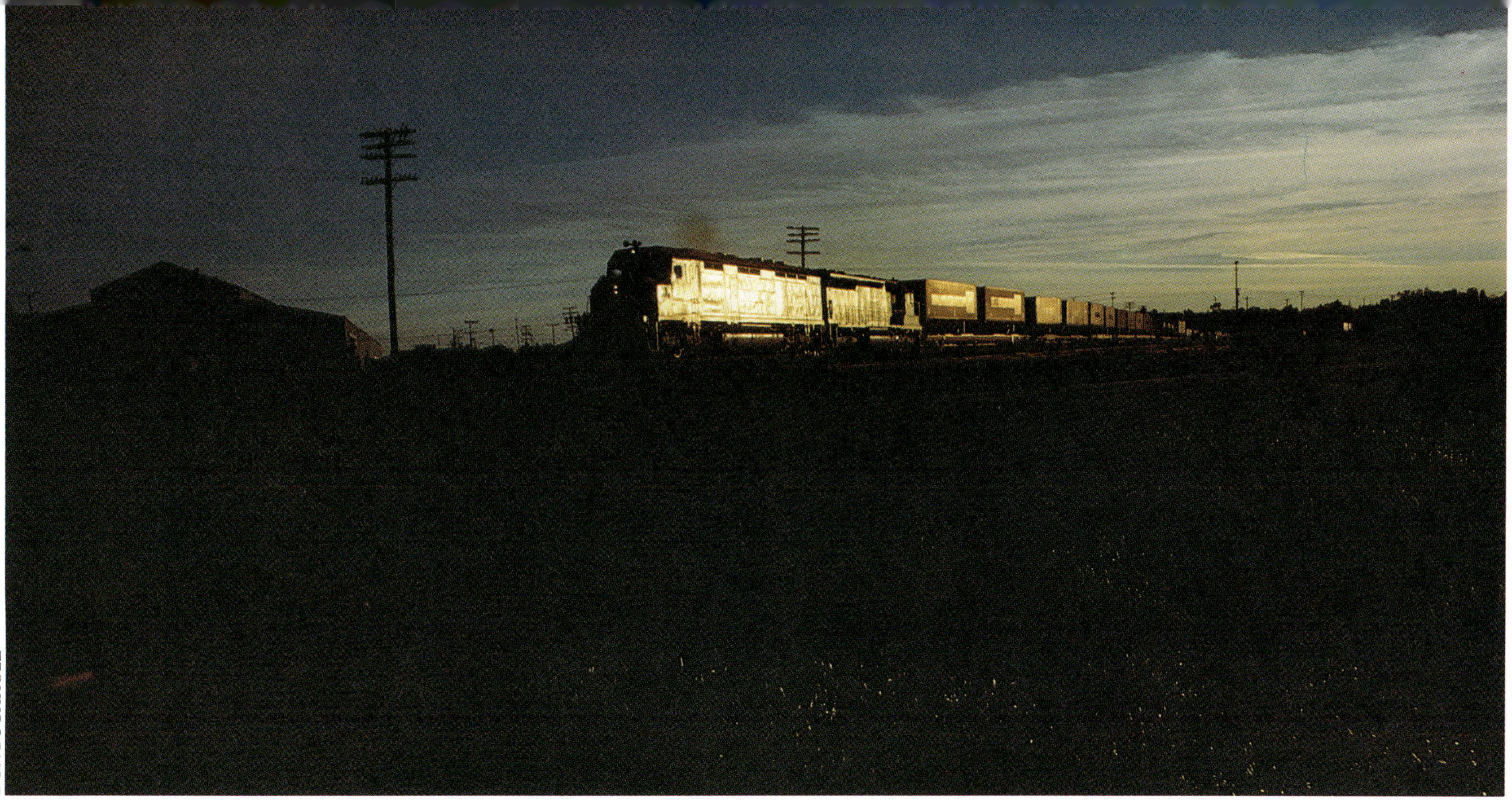

DON BUCHHOLZ

The golden play of light in the East Bay in late afternoon penetrates the surfaces of objects, revealing the planes and layers of underlying metal. We see the effect on a Santa Fe pig train as it departs from the terminal at Richmond headed east toward the darkness of the Central Valley.

Nine hundred twenty-five miles west of Salt Lake City, the mainline rails of Western Pacific end at the West Oakland barge slip, bathed in golden light at the edge of San Francisco Bay. Freight cars were barged across the bay to San Francisco until the late 1970s when agreements were made with SP to forward them by rail.

At Castro Point, near Richmond, the aged metal of Yosemite Valley #107 combine and SP switcher #1269 reflect the sun setting over San Pablo Bay.

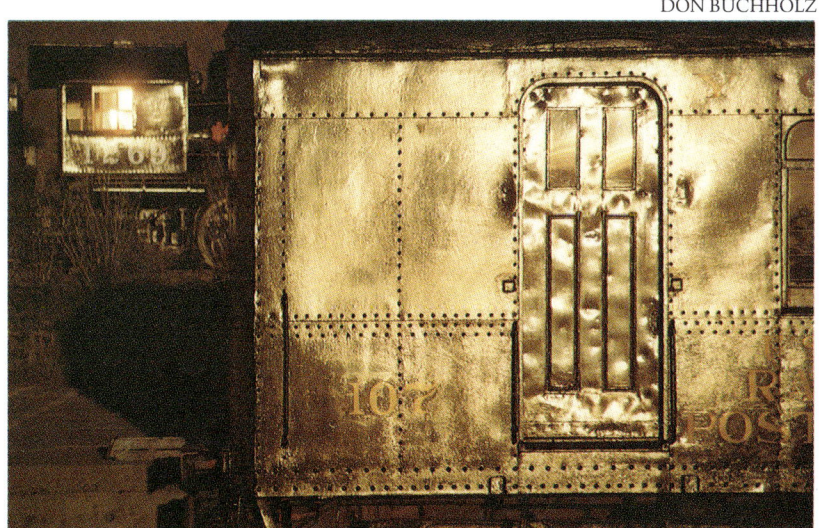

Southern Pacific switcher 2605 (opposite) heads east toward Davis with a local freight in the late glow of sunset. Tom Savio's flash illuminates the reflectorized numbers.

The scary but interesting red volcanic sunsets (left) returned to Northern California in the summer of 1983. We see the SP Spanish-style depot at Davis illuminated fiery red after departure of the westbound Spirit of California.

The Union Pacific throws a party at Portola in June 1983 for its Western Pacific employees. WP-lettered GP40 #3522 helps provide power for the family train rides.

© THOMAS R. SAVIO 1983

© THOMAS R. SAVIO 1983

Santa Fe's San Francisco switching crew works the SP interchange south of Fourth and Townsend. The state's last rail barge service links this Santa Fe outpost with the mainline at Richmond.

While San Franciscans enjoy sunny winter days after a storm, it is not unusual for heavy snow to continue falling 200 miles east in the Sierra Nevada. On the west side of the mountains Dick Dorn catches a big SP double-ended rotary set working down the grade through Yuba Pass.

SHIRLEY BURMAN   CALIFORNIA STATE RAILROAD MUSEUM

SHIRLEY BURMAN

The incredible red cab-forward (above left) "swallowing up" Ken Yeo is not an SP attempt to scare the Hell out of drunk drivers, but a phase of restoration of the #4294 by the California State Railroad Museum in Sacramento.

Artist Kevin Bunker (above) combines work with pleasure outside the Museum, painting banners on Short Line Enterprises #8 for its 1983 trip to the Northern Pacific centennial in Montana.

Thousands of fans (opposite) were delighted by the 1981 Pacific Coast tour of SP's #4449, seen at Grass Lake on the train's southbound run for the opening of the California Railroad Museum.

OPPOSITE: DON BUCHHOLZ

A late sun highlights a westbound Western Pacific BN pool train (left) dropping down off the High Line into Keddie with the motive power "rainbow" typical of this pre-merger period.

Everyone is surprised by the detour operation in March 1983, which sees Santa Fe operating through the Feather River Canyon. This westbound detour train descends the canyon near Merlin, having gotten onto Union Pacific rails near Barstow for the long run to Stockton via Salt Lake City. Closure of Tehachapi Pass for more than a week and continued heavy storms on Donner Pass create this rare event.

DICK DORN PHOTOS

The typeface used in this book is Trump Medieval
Typesetting: Freedmen's Organization, Los Angeles
Color Separations: Reco Color, Burbank, California
Printing: G. R. Huttner Litho, Burbank, California
Design and Layout: Bill Bradley